DIY: Remodel My Life

Jon Fuller

"It takes half your life before you realize that life is a do-it-yourself project."

—Napoleon Hill

Copyright © 2016 Jon Fuller

All rights reserved.

ISBN: 1-63390-047-9
ISBN-13: 978-1-63390-047-9

DEDICATION

This book is dedicated to the struggles that I have had in my life. Had it not been for the need to tear down the old and create the new, I never would have been in a position to help others do the same. I am thankful for the struggle, for that created the desire in me to lay a stronger foundation, build stronger structures, and create what God had always intended.

CONTENTS

	Acknowledgments	i
1	Build Your Model	Pg 1
2	The Contract	Pg 21
3	Demolition	Pg 35
4	Assess the New Framework	Pg 47
5	Repair the Structure	Pg 56
6	Sheetrock—The Canvas	Pg 69
7	Color My Future	Pg 80
8	Set the Final Path	Pg 87
9	Clean Up	Pg 97
10	Warranty Work	Pg 107
	About The Author	Pg 115

ACKNOWLEDGMENTS

I would like to thank my family for supporting me through the process of putting this book together. I would like to thank my coach for pushing me, interviewing me, working with me, and helping me to achieve my dream of writing a book. Thank you Jody Holland! I would like to thank my graphic designer, Mike Grigsby, for the multiple revisions of the cover. Most of all, I would like to thank my God for giving me a dream to help people remodel both their homes and their lives!

1 BUILD YOUR MODEL

"It takes half your life before you discover life is a do-it-yourself project."
—Napoleon Hill

The great commonality of people who have accomplished success in this life is that they have first encountered struggle. They have been hit, kicked, tackled, and challenged by what the world has to offer, and still decided to get back up one more time. They have been pushed around and still kept moving forward. They have built a model of success founded on the principle that no matter what life has thrown at you, or what has happened, they can still remodel. They can still choose what comes next and what life will be like for them. You have started down a path that leads to a new you. You have begun the journey that leads to what you always knew you could be, but have not brought into reality before. You, my friend, are about to start your own life remodel! I am so glad that I get to be a part of the journey, for my gift is being able to restructure the reality that you are in until it becomes the reality that you desire. Welcome to whom you always could have been! Welcome to the new you!

Creating The Model

One of the great challenges of life is to create a model of what we want. We look around at others and want what they have. We crave the relationships that they have. We want the success that they have. We want because we believe that we lack. God has placed inside of you a desire to reach your potential. Just as Max Lucado discussed in his book, *On The Anvil*, we must be purified and refined in order to be the best version of ourselves. We are thrust into the fire, pounded on, and reshaped until what remains is the very best of what we have to offer this world. Every journey has its struggles. If we focus on the struggle, however, many of us will walk away from the journey. Instead, we must focus on the end game. We must focus on the vision of what could be, in order to see past the struggle. Take your eyes off of the obstacles and focus on the prize. What is in store for you is worth so much more than you could have ever imagined!

When I am working with a customer to create the right house for them, I always have them start with a vision for where they want to go. If they don't have a model, I can't create a map for them. It is the model that lays the groundwork for building their dream. The model allows us to evaluate where we are, where we want to go, and what it will take to get there. The model gives us what we need so we can order the right materials, recruit the right help, and begin stepping in the right direction.

The same is true for our lives. We have to decide what we want. To decide is to listen to God's pull on our life and then to act on it. The desire for something more was given to you from God. You were created for success, for greatness, for creating a positive impact in this world. Your desires are there for a reason. They are there because they hold within them the capacity for your greatness. Abraham Maslow, who was one of the key creators of the positive psychology movement, once said, "If you intentionally become less than you are capable of being, then I warn you; you will be unhappy for the rest of your life." You have always known this. You have always known that there was something more for you. Now is your time to decide you will move forward. Now is your time to cut off the other options. The word "decide" comes from the Latin word *de-caedere*, which means, to cut off from. *De* is "off" and *caedere* is "to cut." Once you decide to move forward on this journey, you will literally cut off the old version of yourself and embrace the new reality. When a remodel of your home is done, it is as if the old is completely gone. When done right, people look at your house, and only see the new. They will believe the old was never there and that you are living in the house that was always intended. Your new life—that is the one that people will look at and say, "OF COURSE!" They will see that it is what you were always intended to be. Now, let's get started!

Building your model requires you to be fully honest about who you are and where you are going. It requires your commitment. It requires that you let go of the old version of yourself and choose to move forward. This cannot be done *for* you. It is your choice and only your choice. I will guide you, but I cannot drag you into you. If you desire to live fully into your potential, to let go of the past, to embrace the possibilities of the future, and to live the full and abundant life that God intends for you, please write "AMEN" below this paragraph. Go ahead, it's alright to write in the book. It demonstrates that this journey is yours and that you are on board.

I am in! _____ (Amen)

There are five components of building a model that are critical. They are:

1. What is the blueprint? (Big 5)
2. What is the purpose?
3. What is the budget?
4. What is the vision?
5. What is the timeline?

BLUEPRINT

Within each of us is a blueprint of belief which is guiding all we do. Within each of us is an unconscious blueprint that has been adopted, adjusted, and accepted throughout our life. Very few people are aware of the fact that this blueprint is determining what happens in our relationships, what happens in our businesses, what happens in our financial life, what happens in our spiritual life, what happens in all of our life! The blueprint itself is what we are built upon.

The question of "Who Am I" has been asked by virtually everyone at some point in their lives. They have wondered if they had what it took to be great. They have wondered if they were truly called. They have wondered if being successful made them less connected to God. This world has worked hard to program people for mediocrity. It has worked to take away that spark of genius God has placed inside of them. It has beaten them, challenged them and tried to tell them that God did not want them to succeed, or that they were somehow less of a Christian if they did succeed in life. I am here to tell you that you can simply change your blueprint if you want to. You can evaluate the blueprint for your life and determine if it is the one you intended, then order up the one that fulfills both your desires and your purpose. But—and this is a big but—you must acknowledge what blueprint is guiding your life right now.

The blueprint of your life is running on a loop. Your beliefs, which operate at a subconscious level, are creating your thoughts. Your thoughts, which operate both subconsciously and consciously, are creating your behaviors. Your behaviors, which you are acting out, are creating the results that you are achieving in life. You, my friend, are in complete control of you. You are who you are and where you are because of the beliefs you have accepted, the thoughts in your head, the behaviors you have chosen, and the results you have achieved. Trust me on this one; you are achieving exactly what you are believing…no more and no less.

B – T – B – R (Belief – Thought – Behavior – Result)

What are your beliefs about success, about money, about rich people? These are important questions because your blueprint, or the basis of your belief, is what is determining exactly what you have in your life right now. So let's go through a few biblically misinterpreted verses that might be holding you back, and let's begin to shape your blueprint to work for you instead of against you.

Many believers base their view of money, which is directly correlated to success, on 1 Timothy 6:10, which states:

> For the love of mammon before the love of God is a pathway to all kinds of evil.

Or, as you have likely heard it in church:

> For the love of money is the root of all evil.

The confusion comes with the syntax of the presentation. It is not money that is evil. It never was money that was evil. Money is just a tool, the same as a hammer or a nail or a screwdriver, or a drill. The verse, in its origin, simply said that if you put money before God, then you are on the path to the wrong blueprint. In fact, the verse itself, in its origin, simply states that it is *a* pathway to evil, not *the* pathway to evil. Also, "mammon" was the original word, which means "stuff" or "possessions" and not "money" itself. Paul never said that money was evil. In fact, the Bible talks about the value of money multiple times. Psalms 112:3 describes the man who fears the Lord in this way: "Wealth and riches are in his house, and his righteousness endures forever." This doesn't sound like God hates rich people. This sounds like God blesses righteous people with riches. Abraham was "rich in livestock, in silver, and in gold" (Genesis 13:2). Job was "the greatest of all people of the East" (Job 1:3). Solomon "surpassed all the kings of the earth in wisdom and riches" (1 Kings 10:23).

It should be obvious that God doesn't despise money. In fact, he gives it to those he believes have found their purpose and are living according to the design that God has given them. He gives it to believers who will use it to make a difference in this world. Jabez is an example of someone who understood how to claim his birthright as a believer. Jabez cried out to the God of Israel, "Oh, that You would bless me and enlarge my territory! Let your hand be with me and keep me from harm, so that I will be free from pain. And God granted his request" (1 Chronicles 4:10). God wants you to live into your purpose. He wants you to pursue the desires of your heart, those that He has given you. He wants you to shed your limiting beliefs about the potential that you possess, to give up fear, and to charge forward in the knowledge that you are loved and protected.

Philippians 4:13 says, "I can do all things through Christ

who strengthens me." What does the word "all" mean to you? Does it mean some things, only on a Thursday, with the winds out of the south, at no more than 4.7 miles per hour? Or, does it mean what God intended? Does it truly mean ALL? The only beliefs that are holding you back in your life are the ones that you have accepted and adopted from this world. God's power can and will be made manifest in you when you choose to let go of the old blueprint and embrace your potential. This is not a gradual transformation of your potential. It is a radical transformation that has always been dormant inside of you, waiting for you to let go of those limiting and ungodly beliefs about what you lack.

Marianne Williamson said it best:

"Our deepest fear is not that we are inadequate. Our deepest fear is that we are powerful beyond measure. It is our light, not our darkness that most frightens us. We ask ourselves, 'Who am I to be brilliant, gorgeous, talented, fabulous?' Actually, who are you not to be? You are a child of God. Your playing small does not serve the world. There is nothing enlightened about shrinking so that other people won't feel insecure around you. We are all meant to shine, as children do. We were born to make manifest the glory of God that is within us. It's not just in some of us; it's in everyone. And as we let our own light shine, we unconsciously give other people permission to do the same. As we are liberated from our own fear, our presence automatically liberates others."

What blueprint will you choose to build your life with? Will you choose to accept the limitations of this world? Or will you join me by embracing all of the potential that God has placed inside of you? In my coaching program, I dig deep into who a person is at their core and what limitations they have placed on themselves. By peeling back the layers of limitations and tossing them aside, I help people to reveal the core of who they truly are and embrace all that they are capable of doing. I help people live into God's blueprint instead of their own. Your blueprint was simply laid on top of God's. Get rid of it. Toss it aside. Reveal the full potential that has always been there!

PURPOSE

"The purpose of life is not to be happy. It is to be useful, to be honorable, to be compassionate, to have it make some difference that you have lived and lived well."
—Ralph Waldo Emerson

One of the exercises that I have done with people is to have them write down the things they love to do, that fill them with passion, that drive them forward. I have them think of what lights a fire in them so bright that they would still do it, with or without pay. I have them think of something that they love. Finding your purpose is a process of understanding the potential of your life.

Your purpose statement should have three key elements in it. First, it should not be more than one sentence long. Second, it should be easily understood by a fifth grader. Third, you should be able to share it with people, even under pressure. This means you will need to practice it, and practice it, and practice it. These elements are what make the purpose statement work.

KISMIF: Keep It Simple, Make It Fulfilling! The reason for making your purpose statement only one sentence long is that you need to be able to share it with anyone at any time in under 10 seconds. By making it one sentence long, it is easily understood. It makes sense to people when you share it because it makes sense to you. A few examples of purpose statements that have truly impacted our world are:

"Preserve the Union"	Abraham Lincoln
"End the Depression"	Franklin D Roosevelt
"Show mercy and compassion to the dying"	Mother Teresa

I want you to think about who you are at your core. Think about the model of who you desire to be remembered as. Get that image in your mind clearly. Now, we are about to do several exercises that will help reveal to you what your purpose in life truly is.

List five positive things about yourself.

_____

_____

_____

_____

_____

List three positive things your friends say about you.

_____

_____

_____

Make a list of 5 action verbs that you like the best.
Examples would be love, build, coach, teach, preach

_____

_____

_____

_____

_____

If you could only keep one of the verbs listed above as a descriptor of what you want for your life, which one would you keep and which ones would you eliminate? Go ahead and get rid of each of the verbs that is less important to you, until you have narrowed it down to only one.

Now, make a list of values that you either do stand for or desire to be remembered for standing for. Some examples are things like service, excellence, drive, learning, faith, creativity, potentiality, etc. Make a list of 5 values that you identify with.

_____

_____

_____

_____

_____

Now for the tough part…Go through the list of values and determine which of them you can and will give up, keeping only one or two values as absolutes from the list. I realize that this can be tough, but it is important to evaluate each of the values in your life and choose which are your absolutes and which simply sound good on paper. Those are the ones you think others would want for you instead of the ones you simply *have* to have in your life.

The final piece to this puzzle is to write down five causes that inspire you, excite you, drive you forward, or ways that you know in your gut in which you wish to have an impact on the world in a positive way. Examples of this could be revealing people's potential, feeding the hungry, creating opportunity, growing minds, etc. Write down five causes you believe in.

_____

_____

_____

_____

_____

Okay, this is the last elimination. Now, go through and determine which causes you could and would give up. Keep giving up causes until you get down to the one and only cause that you would not ever and could not ever give up, no matter what.

Let's add it all up and see what we have.

My purpose is _____ (cause)
and I _____ (verb)
because of _____ (value).

As an example:
My purpose is to help people remodel their lives and I pour into people because of my desire to unlock their potential.

BUDGET

Emerson, in his essay on *The Law of Compensation*, helps us to understand that anything we desire in this life requires us to be willing to spend something to get something. This immutable law has kept over 90% of people from living into their potential in life. It has reduced many a person to the level of accepting whatever life handed to them. Napoleon Hill in his book, *Think and Grow Rich*, tells us that action is the bridge between our burning desire and the attainment of that desire.

When I am working with a homeowner to remodel their house, I have to know what they are willing to give, in order to get what they want. If they are unwilling to pay the price that is required of them, then they are never going to have the end result they indicated that they wanted. For me, this is the "Get Real" round of your self-inspection. It is the moment of the truth. It is the pivot point of whether or not you will ever be what and who you were intended to be.

In Luke 15: 11-32, Jesus tells the story of the prodigal son. He tells how the younger son squanders the father's wealth (his potential), but eventually returns home, desiring to simply be one of his father's servants. The father instructs his other servants to bring one of his finest robes, not a ratty and torn one, but one of his finest robes to put around his son. He instructs his servants to kill the fatted calf, which is the one that was raised with the most care to be ready for a great feast. The older son, upset with all of this, tells his father that he has not even offered him "a skinny goat." The mentality of the older son at that point was one of wanting the minimal in life and receiving the minimal in life. Jesus taught that one must have a "fatted calf" mentality about fulfilling one's purpose and not a "skinny goat" mentality. If you are unwilling to give what it takes to achieve your destiny, then you are unwilling to achieve your destiny. It is your choice and it is now decision time.

Please take a minute to write out what you are giving up and what it could potentially cost you if you choose not to give what is required of you for the attainment of your destiny.

_____

_____

_____

_____

_____

_____

_____

Now, take a minute and write out what you could potentially have if you do achieve your destiny in this life. In other words, what are all of the benefits that you can think of, in relation to achieving what you were put here on this earth to achieve?

_____

_____

_____

_____

_____

_____

_____

Now, for the bonus round: What are you willing to give in order to get what you desire? What are you willing to sacrifice to achieve your destiny? Will you give time, resources, emotional energy, sleep, if necessary? What will you give?

_____

_____

_____

_____

_____

_____

_____

Congratulations! You now know what your budget actually is and why that is your budget. Read back through this a time or two and determine whether or not you would be able to achieve your destiny on the budget that you have described. If you cannot achieve your destiny on what you are willing to give, you will have to make a decision. Will you reduce your destiny or increase your budget? Those are your only two choices in the matter!

VISION

"Vision is the art of seeing what is invisible to others."
—Jonathan Swift

Your vision for your life is based on accepting the present truth of the future reality. You must create inside of yourself a burning desire to move toward something. At the same time, you must hold the truth of the future in your mind, as if already attained.

So many times in our lives, we live as if we will never make it to that ubiquitous point in the future called success. We indicate that next year we will save for retirement, next year we will get ready to send our kids to college, next year we will take action towards our dreams. There is not next year. There is only the present in the subconscious mind. If you see your success as only in the future, then you will live as if that day will never be here. We are called to cast a vision that we simply live into. We must see who we are as our future *now*. I do realize that sentence sounds a little strange. The truth of the matter is that your mind can be a little strange. Your mind needs to see you, right now, as the potential that is within you. It needs to see a picture of what you look like as the amazing successful person that God always intended.

You need to be able to look one year into the future and write out, in present tense, exactly what you have already achieved. You need to paint a picture for your mind to live into. You need to be the success you were designed to be and not simply think about "some day" or "one day." Your future is now. Your remodel begins today! Take five minutes and describe in present tense exactly what you will have accomplished in the past year. An example sentence is:

DIY My Life

Today is _____ (exactly one year from today) I speak for groups of 1,000+ on a weekly basis, sharing my insights on success and remodeling life. I have 32,378 followers on my R U Real Podcast. I live in a 4200-square-foot home with an amazing back yard. My wife and kids are happy and healthy. My book has sold 81, 222 copies.

Now, write out at least 10 sentences that paint a word picture of your current achievements at exactly one year in the future. Write it in the present tense because your mind only works in the present tense. It does not see the future or the past at a subconscious level. You are impacting your blueprint and changing your reality here!

_____

_____

_____

_____

_____

_____

_____

_____

_____

_____

_____

_____

_____

_____

_____

_____

_____

_____

_____

_____

_____

TIMELINE

Now we do a little planning and mapping out of actions. In order to achieve the things that you have planned for one year from today, to begin achieving the destiny for which you were designed, you have to map out what you will do, by when, and with what result.

Make a list of the things you have achieved in the last year (one year from today) and then give each of them an amount of time that it would take to achieve them. You are budgeting your time, which allows you to have an accurate timeline of actions to take in order to reach these objectives.

If you don't create a budget of time, you will likely spend your time on other things that are not moving you toward your destiny. This is really important! I would encourage you to even overestimate the amount of time it might take to get the perfect results that you desire.

Item Achieved	Amount of Time it Will Take
_____	_____
_____	_____
_____	_____
_____	_____
_____	_____
_____	_____
_____	_____
_____	_____
_____	_____
_____	_____
_____	_____

The next step is to play in reverse in order to attain your future present. You will need to map out how much time you can allocate on a daily, weekly, monthly basis toward the attainment of your destiny. You must be willing to budget your time in order to achieve the one-year timeline for your growth and success. Take out your calendar right now and block off time to do the things that are necessary in order to achieve the objectives that are a part of your vision. If you are unwilling to schedule the necessary time, you are going back on what you said you were willing to give up in order to have what you were always supposed to have. I don't think you want to live your life un-remodeled. I think you picked this book up because you know that now is the time to begin taking action and living into the life you were meant to have. Seriously, stop reading and put time on your calendar equivalent to the amount of time necessary to achieve all of your vision!

I will commit the required time in order to have the ordained life!

Signed: _____

This is only the beginning, but I do realize this chapter was truly challenging to lots of folks. I want to let you know how proud I am of you and the choice you have made to live into all that God intended for your life. You were intended for greatness. You were intended to accomplish things that bring glory to God's Kingdom and that shine as a beacon of hope for others. You living into your potential places you in a position of influence. People are desperate for an example of the fullness of God's glory. Thank you for taking this journey with me and thank you for choosing to live a remodeled life!

2 THE CONTRACT

"Desire is the key to motivation, but it's determination and commitment to an unrelenting pursuit of your goal—a commitment to excellence that will enable you to attain the success that you seek."
—Mario Andretti

Everything in life is just a conversation until the day that there is a commitment. The contract is what compels us to move forward to what we know is right, to live in the manner that will create our vision of our future. When we put it all on the line, we are saying that we actually want our vision, our model of the future, to replace our existing picture. There are several things that hold people back at this point. There are also several things that can propel us forward.

Throughout our lives, we are challenged to put our actions where our mouths are. We are challenged to do something instead of just talking about doing something. When we create a contract for a remodel, we are committing that we are ready to take action and make the world a better place. We are committing that we are ready to live into the purpose for which we were designed. For years, I have listened to people indicate that "some day" they were going to do something incredible with their lives. I have listened to them say that they wanted to start a business, or start a ministry, or cultivate an idea, or start a family, or start something, all without the action portion of success. My question to them has been: "When is some day for you?" It is the "some day" definition that makes the biggest difference, because it is the component which determines whether today is the day you take action or whether you leave your dream of who you can be on the shelf.

In Mark 1, beginning with Verse 16, Jesus calls his disciples to follow him.

> 16 As Jesus walked beside the Sea of Galilee, he saw Simon and his brother Andrew casting a net into the lake, for they were fishermen. 17 "Come, follow me," Jesus said, "and I will send you out to fish for people." 18 At once they left their nets and followed him.
> 19 When he had gone a little farther, he saw James son of Zebedee and his brother John in a boat, preparing their nets. 20 Without delay he called them, and they left their father Zebedee in the boat with the hired men and followed him. (Bible Gateway, 2016)

Jesus didn't say, "Hey guys, when you get done fishing and you can't find any other excuses for not taking action, it would be awesome if you followed me and saved the world." He told them to come, right now, and follow him. When we sign the contract to move forward, we are signing a contract to move forward *now*, not at some nebulous time in the future.

In Matthew 8:21-22, Jesus refutes the excuses that

were being brought up.
> [21] Another disciple said to him, "Lord, first let me go and bury my father."
> [22] But Jesus told him, "Follow me, and let the dead bury their own dead." (Bible Gateway, 2016)

During that time, "the dead" were considered to be the individuals who were elderly, not actually dead. Jesus was telling the would-be disciple that you will always be able to come up with an excuse if you try. Instead, do not let anything stand in the way of you pursuing your destiny in Him. He was telling them to take action now! Forget the excuses! Take action.

When we create the contract, we are doing that very thing and it requires setting our mind on the right path to move us forward and fulfill our purpose in life. We have to be ready to face the things that could keep us from our purpose, though. We must be ready to uncover those beliefs that would hold us back. For one of the disciples, it was the idea that he needed to live out the life of a parent before he took action. That is an extreme enough example where Jesus wanted us to know that your excuse about not being able to take action because it is "uncomfortable" is not going to cut it. To remodel you, you have to let go of your excuses, your limiting beliefs, and any other limitations that you have placed on yourself; then embrace the future of who you can and should be.

The limiting beliefs that we have in our lives are what often freeze us in our tracks and prevent us from taking action. When I am looking at a house and I know a wall is already in place, but it isn't where the homeowner wants it, I simply design what it would take to move the wall. I never look at them and say, "Oh man, that wall is already there so we will just have to work around it. We can't remove it." The truth is that *anything* is possible. Some things take more work and more planning than others, but they are still possible. If you are willing to leave the boats of your security in who you have been in the past, then you will be able to set sail in a new direction, for a new shore, on your new adventure.

The first thing you must do, however, is recognize the beliefs that could be holding you back. Are you waiting on a person in your life to make their changes first? Are you waiting for the time to be just right? Are you waiting on it to… (fill in the blank with your own excuse here)? When you are waiting, you are not in the contract period and you are not taking action.

Moses tried to tell God that he was not right to follow the purpose for which he was created. When he was first called, he said, "But, but, but, but, I, I, st, stu, studder." He had a speech impediment, yet he was being called to be the voice of God. I even wonder if God didn't *have* to speak to Moses with a burning bush because he might not have listened if He just showed up and gave him the Commandments. I would like for you to make a list of up to 10 excuses for why you can't, shouldn't, or might not take action.

Excuses: _____

_____

_____

_____

_____

_____

Those excuses are the limiting beliefs that have been keeping you from achieving your destiny. They are the foolish pretenses used as justification that have prevented you from success. I heard a story recently about Lancelot traveling the countryside and challenging the warriors of his land to fight him with a sword and see if they could win. His quest was to find great knights that could live by the three principles of battle whom he could raise up to greatness. Within a village, he would shout out his challenge and get the men to gather. He would shake a bag full of gold pieces and say that any many that could beat him with a sword could have the bag of gold. He told them that he was looking for warriors that could join him in defending the king and the kingdom. One rather tall and strong man stepped up and raised his sword to do battle with Lancelot. They fought hard against one another until right at the moment the man thought he was about to win, Lancelot disarmed him with a single move and placed his blade precariously at the man's throat. The man yielded and Lancelot had won...again. He then asked the man if he wished to learn, and the man did indeed want to know the secret of success. Lancelot said that there are three steps to victory:

1. Develop your skill with a fervor for victory.
2. Wait until the most heated part of the battle to strike the winning blow.
3. Do not care whether you live or die.

The man's face sank, for he knew that he cared greatly whether he lived or died. Lancelot turned and walked away in search of someone who could actually be a great warrior and was worthy of being a Knight of the Round

Table, for that man was not the one.

Think about what it takes to be successful. When you spend your time thinking about what the potential cost of moving forward would be instead of being in the moment, where peace and action come together, then you are living like the man who was unworthy of the calling. If the disciples had told Jesus that they were unable to go right now because they had some other fish to fry first, they would never have changed the world. I want you to write a few sentences on each of your limiting beliefs, or excuses, that you listed before. I want you to write a sentence explaining what it will cost you if you choose not to move forward. Then I want you to write what you will benefit if you do move forward. By outlining the pain of not taking action and the pleasure of taking action, you will position yourself to be motivated for success instead of being motivated for failure.

Excuse: _____

Why I must take action (pain/pleasure): _____

_____

_____

_____

_____

Why I must take action (pain/pleasure): _____

_____

_____

DIY My Life

_____

_____

Why I must take action (pain/pleasure): _____

_____

_____

_____

Why I must take action (pain/pleasure): _____

_____

_____

_____

Why I must take action (pain/pleasure): _____

_____

_____

_____

Why I must take action (pain/pleasure): _____

_____

_____

_____

_____

Why I must take action (pain/pleasure): _____

_____

_____

_____

_____

Why I must take action (pain/pleasure): _____

_____

_____

_____

_____

Why I must take action (pain/pleasure): _____

_____

_____

_____

_____

Why I must take action (pain/pleasure): _____

_____

_____

_____

_____

What holds most of us back is the choice *not* to accept the forgiveness of God. We think that we are not worthy because we have sinned. Sin is the willful separation from God, yet that is the illusion that brings no joy and no fulfillment. It is in the return to God, the embracing of the contract to move forward, that we eliminate the guilt of past sins. It is in that choice, that commitment, that we find our path to peace and wholeness.

Once you have addressed the limiting beliefs in your life, you will then be ready to move your life onto a new pathway. The contract God gave us is that He sent his son Jesus to save us from our sins. Over and over again, I have reminded people that either God meant what he said in contract with us, that we are saved from sin and death because of Jesus Christ, or He didn't. Since God doesn't break His promises, since His contracts are good, then I choose to believe. I believe I am saved from separation from God as long as I accept the connection. God has laid out His contract to us. He wants the best for us. He does not want us to suffer or fail. He wants us to succeed.

In Genesis, God tells Abraham that both Jews and Gentiles would be blessed, that his offspring—us, the people of the earth—are called into blessing. Just like Abraham and Sarah's story, though, we must follow the contract of God in order to receive what was intended for us. If we do not live into the beliefs we were given, then we create a mess. It is fear, not hate, that binds us into the wrong life. It is fear that God didn't mean what He said that limits our beliefs. That is the reason that we choose—yes, choose—to live a life of limitations instead of a life of abundance. God put forth that he wants the best for you. He gave you a purpose, a brain, and abilities or talents. What you do with it from there is up to you. He doesn't do it for you. He simply outlines the path and prepares the way. His side of the contract is already done. He wrote up the agreement that He wanted the best for you. He wants you to live into your purpose and find success. Now, will you leave your boats, let the dead bury the dead, be willing to sacrifice what is necessary, and be willing to act and continue acting until you achieve your purpose?

If you are willing to commit, then your next step is to get rid of the old associations that you have had. You are the average of the five closest people/relationships that you have in life. What is tough for many people is the act of leaving behind the people who would keep you from achieving what you were intended to achieve. Some of your "friends" don't want you to be successful. They want you to be like them. When you associate with people who live by their limitations, it can be very intimidating to them to have one of their associates move forward in life. As my life began to change and I embraced that God had a destiny for me, I stopped doing some of the things that I had done in the past. I was not asked to "give them up." I *wanted* to give them up because they represented the old me and not the potential me. When I stopped drinking, my friends who were drinkers became uncomfortable around me. When I cleaned up my language, some of my friends didn't want to be around me because I no longer talked like them.

When you want to succeed in life, you seek out right associations and you are willing to walk away from the wrong ones. The contract to remodel your life says that you must be willing to move a few structural walls around as well as some non-supportive walls. You cannot have the blessings that were intended, the remodeled you, unless you commit to give up the old you, the unremodeled you. If you are willing to let the old pass away and have the new come, I would like for you to write the following sentence in this book. Rewrite in your own handwriting and sign the following:

I, (your full name), am committing right now, to move forward with remodeling my life into the full potential that God has placed inside of me. I will take action every day, give up the old version of me, and become the new version of me. Then sign and date it.

_____

_____

_____

_____

_____

_____

_____

_____

The next step you must take is to begin programming your heart and your mind with the right inputs. If you focus on the dust and destruction of a remodel then you begin to build up negative energy toward the end product. If you focus on the beauty and majesty of your remodel, then you focus on the here and now of the action as well as the potential of the future. What you focus on is your choice. One of the easy ways to stay focused on the right components of success is to put good things into your mind. Reading your Bible, reading books that build you up, hanging out with people who want to see the potential you in all of it's glory, those are the inputs you need now. We were instructed to fellowship with believers. We need to study the Word of God in order to understand the blueprint that He has given us for life. It is the blueprint that contains the design and hope for our future. Within that blueprint, you see that there are three steps you must follow in order to get this remodel going:

1. You must have a burning desire to move forward. This means reminding yourself of what you were put here to do. One of the easiest ways to do this is to commit to the journey. If you commit, then you are deciding that there are not other alternatives. In a remodel, we don't outline what we *might* do. Instead, we outline what we *will* do! Your desire to move forward must burn inside of you. It must be so bright that others can't help but come and see what is happening. That burning desire attracts the help you need and inspires others to take action as well.
2. You must back your desire with faith. In rappelling, you can believe that your rope will keep you safe, or that your team will be ready to protect you, but you don't have faith until you go over the edge of the cliff and prove it. Faith is the willingness to act in the face of fear or threat. It is the willingness to jump off the edge of the new adventure and know in your heart and your mind that God is with you. When you study the word of God, you find that God actually wants the best for you. He wants you to be successful and

remodeled into your potential. He has signed His contract with the blood of His son. He is simply awaiting your signature to get started. He is incredibly serious. Are you?
3. You must be filled with action. When a person prays and then does nothing, he is living in a one-sided contract. When I remodel a house, I am committing to doing the work and the homeowner is committing to pay for the work. If either of us fails to act on our part, then the remodel does not work. It is the same thing with your purpose. You must be willing to act. God has already paid the price with his Son. He gave you a purpose. Will you act? Will you do your part or will you back out on God and refuse to live into the remodeled life that was intended for you?

God was a builder! He was not a waiter. He did not wait for instruction from others. He took action in every situation. He found the people to help Him, the people who had a purpose to fulfill. He then equipped them with the tools and resources to move forward. He relied on those people to do their part, though. Moses had to raise his staff to part the waters. His part was not exceedingly difficult but God did not act unless Moses was willing to do his part as well. God has laid out a contract to remodel your life and help you enjoy the glory of His presence. He is waiting on you to take action. A burning desire to move forward, filled with faith in the attainment of that desire, and propelled forward with action is what it takes for this contract to be signed. Move forward now with your full commitment to action in the remodel of you. Live into your potential!

I, _____ (write your name), commit right

here and right now to take action every day in order to

_____

_____. I accept that it is my choice as to whether I remodel my life or simply remain the same as I have been, and I will not blame anyone or anything else if I choose not to take action.

Signature: _____

Date: _____

3 DEMOLITION

"The fire exists to purify us, to purge from our lives that which holds us back. Were it not for challenges and struggles, we could never grow into our full potential."
—Jody Holland

Anytime there is a remodel, there are things that simply have to go. There are walls in the wrong place. There are doors that aren't working. There are windows that aren't where we want them. There may even be foundations with cracks in them. No matter what it is, it has to be torn down before it can be built back up.

Why Am I Facing These Challenges? This is a question I have heard person after person after person ask over the years. The day I began helping people find their purpose was the day I figured out that there is no purpose without struggle. When people are given a challenge or when they have to overcome something, they begin to build their muscles related to success. It is the same with a house. When I begin to tear into a house, I am able for the first time to see what needs to be fixed. If I never damage the veneer of the house, I never expose the things that need to be addressed. In the same way, it is the struggle we face that allows us to see what needs to be remodeled.

The very essence of you is challenged by the idea of change. A part of who you are, your underlying identity, is based in the old concepts of you. When you begin to create change in your life, there is a part of you that clings to the old. Matthew 9:17 says:

> [17] And no one puts new wine into old wineskins. For the old skins would burst from the pressure, spilling the wine and ruining the skins. New wine is stored in new wineskins so that both are preserved.

It is natural for people to go back to what they know. They have been conditioned to think, act, and achieve in a way that has put them into the position they are in right now. Each of us is who we are and where we are because of the series of choices we have made. If we want to be someone or somewhere else, we have to make different choices. In order to make a new choice, you must embrace a new set of information and (this is a big and) let go of the old information.

A FEW PEOPLE WHO OVERCAME

Had Walt Disney not been fired from the Kansas City Star for "lacking imagination and having no good ideas," we would not have the Disney empire that we have today.

Had Oprah Winfrey not been publicly fired from her first television job as an anchor in Baltimore for getting "too emotionally invested in her stories," she never would have become the billionaire talk show host, magazine owner, and influencer that she is today.

Had Steven Spielberg not been rejected by the

University of Southern California School of Cinematic Arts multiple times, he would not have jumped into action and created the 27 blockbusters to his credit that have grossed more than 9 billion dollars.

Had Soichiro Honda not been rejected repeatedly by Toyota for his ideas on pistons, not been ostracized by the Japanese business community for his individualism, and not been bombed at his factory in WWII, he would not have created the Piper Cub motorcycle and built the Honda empire. He opened up the U.S. automotive market to Japanese products for the first time and made Japanese cars a force to be reckoned with.

Vera Wang failed to make the 1968 Olympic figure-skating team. She then became an editor at Vogue, but was passed over for the editor-in-chief position. Frustrated with her failure, she decided to design a few wedding gowns at the age of 40. She is now one of the premier designers in the fashion industry with a business worth over 1 billion dollars.

Thomas Edison was told by his teachers that he was "too stupid to learn" and never finished any formal education. He was fired from his job selling candy and newspapers on a train at the age of 11. And yet, he went on to hold over 1,000 patents and "light" the way for others.

J.K. Rowling was a single mom living off welfare when she first began to write. As she penned the first Harry Potter novel, she created a better world for herself as well as for millions of others. In 2004, she became the very first author to become a billionaire as a result of their writing.

One of my Podcast guests, Paul Young, was working

three jobs, and was challenged by his wife to write a book since they could not afford to buy presents for his kids. He wrote the book *The Shack* while riding a train back and forth to one of his jobs. After he made a handful of copies at a local copy store, his friends liked the book and encouraged him to send it out to a publisher. After being rejected over and over and over again, he self-published. That book made him close to 100 million dollars in profit (more than he would have made with a publisher), and gave him a platform to influence.

Theodore Geisel, better known as Dr. Seuss, was rejected by 27 different publishers for his first book. *The Cat In The Hat*, along with other classics like *Green Eggs and Ham*, went on to sell hundreds of millions of copies worldwide and inspire a love for reading in children and adults.

As Christians, we are not required to let go of all of the bad stuff before we are accepted by Christ. We have always been loved and accepted by Him. As Christians, desiring to remodel of our lives, we take hold of the desire to live into the image of a great life, and therefore we choose to let go of our old habits and past beliefs. Demolition is about cleansing ourselves, the same way that you would cleanse your house of anything improper. It is a choice that we make, but nothing moves forward until the choice to demo is a commitment.

Demolition requires the following of us:

1. Embrace the struggle and learn from it.
2. Destroy what is in the way of our DIY success.
3. Expose any structural or foundational issues that might not be otherwise visible.

EMBRACE THE STRUGGLE AND LEARN FROM IT

Whether you are thinking about the tax collector, the murderer, the fishermen, the zealots, or the hot-heads, you are still thinking about one or more of the 12 disciples that helped to spread the Gospel of Jesus Christ throughout the world. When Jesus began putting together his "dream team," he didn't go out and find the purest of the pure and have them provide resumes to be considered amongst the most holy. He didn't look at their lives and say, "Oh man, you guys are jacked up; I could never use you." Instead, time and again, Jesus demonstrated that he could take that which was broken and make it whole. He could take those of us who had struggled and remove the rough edges in order to build us into something beautiful.

When you look at your life and the struggles you have gone through, you are often seeing the bad side of your life without seeing the upside of the struggle. Winston Churchill once said, "Success is the ability to go from one failure to another without loss of enthusiasm." I have tried to imagine what it was like for the disciples when this man, Jesus, who was so obviously different from the rest of the world, invited them to follow Him. He was the Son of God and he was asking quite the motley crew to leave behind their old lives and follow Jesus. I imagine that they were thinking what many of us today still think:

Is this guy crazy? Does he have any idea how bad a person I have been? I have hunted down and bullied people like Him. I have been mean to other people. I have not been a good father/mother. I have not been honest in all of my dealings. I have not tithed 10% of my income to help others. I have not given of my time. I have lied about stuff. I have made up stories to get out of stuff. I have collected money from people that I should not have. I have...I have... (you can fill in the blank)

Whatever your excuse for why God cannot use you, it isn't good enough. The struggles we face help us to understand what we really want in this life. They help us to understand who God is. They give God a chance to demonstrate His love, His grace, His mercy, His remodeling power. They have prepared you for the life that was always there for you. Philippians 4:12-13 says:

> 12 I know what it is to be in need, and I know what it is to have plenty. I have learned the secret of being content in any and every situation, whether well fed or hungry, whether living in plenty or in want. 13 For I can do all things through Christ who gives me the strength.

Often times, people forget Verse 12 in this meditation. Consider that Paul was actually sitting in jail when he wrote this. He was arrested, thrown into a cell, not fed well, no cable TV, no yard time, nothing! He was just sitting there and he had the thought that he was alright because he chose to have peace. Sometimes I think we struggle to remember that we are still okay, even if we are not doing that great outwardly. I do not believe that this is the place God intended for us to stay, but it is a stop along the way to becoming who we could be.

There is a lesson in there for you, for me, for each of us. There is a lesson that we are supposed to learn before we are supposed to move to the next level. For me, the lesson was that God's got this. Even though I was struggling, God had a plan which involved action on my part. When I was in the midst of my own struggles, I cried out to God and asked Him to help me out of the situation. I made a contract with God. I told Him that I would do my part. I would take action and begin to eliminate the things from my life which were holding me back and keeping me from peace. I would do this no matter what! I didn't say that if he would remove the bad from my life, I would begin to believe. I first said that I believed in Him and that I would begin to remove the bad stuff from my life. It started with the commitment and then moved toward action on my part. I asked Him to be a part of my life while I was removing the bad. My relationship with Him was not conditional on Him fixing my life for me.

I think that point is important, because His wholeness is made manifest in our lives when we embrace Him now. It isn't some nebulous point in the future that we will love God. There isn't an "if" in the statement. There is only the fact that we are finally opening up to a relationship with God. God has been standing there, ready to love you, in and through your struggle. He has been waiting for you to allow Him in. You didn't have to go find Him. He was always there in the struggle with you. Embrace the truth that He loves you now and that you have to commit to do your part to change.

When you embrace the struggle and realize that this is the perfect time for you to change yourself, then God's power will multiply your efforts. Without you taking action and making an effort, however, God has nothing to multiply. Anything times zero is zero. You learned that in elementary school. Give God something to work with. Make your commitment to take action in the midst of your struggle and do your part.

DESTROY WHAT IS IN THE WAY OF YOUR DIY SUCCESS

Imagine that you have decided you want to add a beautiful and unique sink into your bathroom. You have looked at what you have and you have realized that it is ugly as heck. You can't stand it. You look at it and you think, "Man, I have got to get rid of that ugly thing because it doesn't match, smells bad, and it is in the way." You realize that it needs to go, but you just starting trying to build a sink on top of it. That doesn't work, does it? You can't put the new on top of the old and think that it is going to look good. In the same way, if your clothes are old and worn out, but you just add a layer on top of them, you don't have the look you... or smell you desire. It is only in removing the old, destroying that which is in your way of becoming who you were meant to be, that your life begins to take shape.

When Jesus called each of the disciples, He instructed them to leave behind the old. He told them that it was time to move forward, which was only possible if they left behind the old. This isn't always easy. Sometimes it means leaving behind your drinking buddies. You will find that people often want to bring you back down instead of building you up, because they know that they are not living right and it feels better for them if you you don't progress either. When people try to stop drinking, try to stop doing drugs, or try to stop gambling, they have to get away from the temptation. When we place ourselves in the midst of temptation, we are the most likely to struggle and to ultimately fail.

If you knew that there was a guy that wanted to beat you up in a certain alley and he did every time you walked down that alley, how many times do you go down the alley? Do you go just once? Do you keep going time and again? Most of us learn on the first try that a new route is a good idea. However, when it comes to finding success in our lives, finding peace, finding joy, we keep going down the alley with the bad guy. One of the first steps for you to succeed would be to put up a barricade to the alley. Then, make sure that you never go down that alley again.

With your house, if you had a wall that smelled bad, had mold on it, or something along those lines, you wouldn't keep that wall in the house. You would destroy the wall! You would get rid of it.

I love to watch remodeling shows. I get some great ideas and learn from other contractors in the process. In each of these shows, the remodel begins with a plan and then moves quickly into tearing out all of the old. It is a joyously aggressive part of the show. They take sledgehammers to the old stuff. They rip and cut and yank and destroy that which is holding them back from creating the new. You have to do the same. You, as the star of your own life remodel, have to put on some gloves and some goggles, and begin to rip away all of the old stuff! Tear out anything and everything that could possibly hold you back. Get rid of the bars, the booze, and anything that leads to backsliding. Get rid of the lies, the lust, and the loose living. Get rid of the people, places, and possibilities of doing bad things. When you first get rid of those things, you are in a starting position for success. When you keep the old in place, you are in a starting position for failure. I am all for the success position myself, not the failure position. How about you?

EXPOSE ANY STRUCTURAL OR FOUNDATIONAL ISSUES THAT MIGHT NOT OTHERWISE BE VISIBLE

Earlier, we talked about the limiting beliefs that could be holding you back. We discussed how these things are deep inside of you. The fact that you have torn away the things that were covering those limiting beliefs over means you are now ready to check the foundational issues of your life. It isn't until you tear away the old that you can see what is really on the inside. Many people will feel that they are unworthy of God's love, even after they tear away the old. They will think that they needed to earn it and after going through the demolition process, they may feel even more strongly about that. I want to step back from the walls and just breathe for a second.

Once I tear out the old sheetrock, rip out the carpet, bust up the tile, and destroy the vanities that were in the way, I can see what needs to be done to make the house really work. In the same way, you wouldn't really know what was going on deep in your heart until you got rid of the things that could prevent you from moving forward. You might feel a bit lonely when your friends stop wanting to hang out with you because you are now on the right track, but take heart…God's best is coming!

If you have some faulty wiring that keeps lighting up the bad parts of your old life, it is time to rewire. If you have a foundation that is cracked and says that you were never good enough, it is time to level that out. It is time to shore up the walls that will protect you from the storms of life. As we see the things that have eaten away at us over the years and kept us from seeing that we were always good enough because we were and are children of God, and we expose the wiring that has short-circuited our success, we can fix them.

People only fix that which they realize is broken. When you were on the wrong path in life, you didn't know it. You only knew that you were on a path. This process you have walked through has allowed you to see the truth about where you were. You can't have the new while holding onto the old. Now that things are exposed, you have to make your next choice. Do you want to move forward or do you want to simply cover things back up? I am going to ask for your commitment again. I need to know. You need to know. God needs to know if you want to embrace the gifts and blessings that He has for you—or do you want to slide back into the old life? Once the next phase of the remodel begins, there is no turning back.

I, _____, am committing right here and right now that I will move forward. I will not go backwards. I want to remove the bad wiring, fix the foundation of who I am, and create something beautiful.

_____
(Signature)

_____
(Date)

Alright, you are in. You are committed to make the changes that are necessary. You are 100% focused on being the best version of yourself possible. You are leaving behind the old and embracing the new. Now for one more tough part. I need you to list out the things that you will never go back to. I need to you list out the bad wiring and wrong foundations that have been keeping you from embracing being a child of God who was and is destined for greatness.

The bad wiring that I will never go back to:

_____

_____

_____

_____

Jon Fuller

4 ASSESS THE FRAMEWORK

The framework is a mystery until the demolition is completed. Our lives are a combination of illusion and cover-up until the sheetrock is removed and the internal structure is exposed. It often takes a coach, an accountability partner, or a trusted leader to help guide us along the right path. When we assess the framework of our lives, just like the framework of a house, we must be willing to live fully exposed. This can be one of the most difficult choices for a person to make because it means letting go of the illusion that we have created for others.

In watching shows on HGTV about flipping houses, you see the number of times that a house looks pretty good, but when the sheetrock is pulled back, the wiring is bad, or there are plumbing issues, or the HVAC needs to go. You see the real story when the façade is gone. You also see the agony on the faces of the new homeowners as they try to decide if it's worth moving forward. They look at the task at hand and try to determine if they have the strength, and resources, and support to keep going. During this time, there are three things that you, as the owner of your brand new life, must do, and there are three keys to making it through the process.

3 Things That You Must Do
1. Use the right inspector.
2. Be completely honest and open.
3. Hold nothing back.

3 Keys to Making it Through the Process
1. Create a burning desire to live the new life that you created in the model stage.
2. Have faith that you are on the right path.
3. Surround yourself with people who want you to succeed.

USE THE RIGHT INSPECTOR

When we are in the middle of becoming who we were always meant to be, it is easy to lose sight of where we have been and why we need to change. In remodeling a house, I have an expert come in after the demolition is done and evaluate the framework of what we have. I have an electrician look at the wiring. I have a plumber look at the plumbing. I have my framer look at the studs and structure. I have people who are gifted in their area of expertise look at the overall structure and makeup of the house.

Think about your life as that framework. It is incredibly easy to slide backwards into using the faulty wiring of our past conditioning, unless we have someone who is willing to be our accountability partner and help us to move forward. This can be done in the form of hiring a life coach, or finding someone from the Bible-based church you are now attending, or from finding a friend who has already walked the path that you are on. Having someone who knows what they are doing and is willing to push, pull, drag, cajole, and inspire you by being honest with you is invaluable.

The inspector who you recruit has to have permission to evaluate most of your life. For example, I had a friend who had struggled with pornography, so he asked me if I would be his accountability partner and have access to a software program which tracked every website he went to and how long he was on the site. This program would send a notification email to me any time he visited a site that might be questionable. He and I would speak once a week about where he was at and we would talk through the challenges of being a godly man in a somewhat ungodly world. It isn't easy to open up to another person and reveal all of the truth about who you are and the choices you have and are making. However, it is one of the most critical things we can do to ensure that we are staying on the right track. You can't have the life you desire if you are chained to the anchor of your past choices! Each of us is more likely to stay on the right path if we know that someone is looking.

BE COMPLETELY HONEST AND OPEN

People who love you will love you in truth. People who don't love you will not really love you either in truth or in a lie. It is the truth, however, which unlocks your ability to be genuinely you. Your happiness in this life doesn't come from wearing the mask that others want to see. It comes from taking off the mask and revealing all of who you are, so you can be all of who you were meant to be. John 8:32 says, "Then you shall know the truth, and the truth shall set you free." You cannot be free from the old version of you until you are willing to embrace that it was an old version.

In trying to become more of the man, woman, father, mother, brother, sister, or any other role you play, you have to admit that you were not always who you could have been. It is our choices that ultimately make up the sum of who we are and it is our choices that either take us where we could be or keep us where we were. If you are completely honest with yourself, you realize what my friend Jody Holland says: "You are who you are and where you are because of the choices you have made. If you want to be someone else or somewhere else, you will make new choices." The reason Alcoholics Anonymous has each person begin with stating their name and the truth that they are an alcoholic is because it is in the admission that you begin to find your freedom.

It can be painful to be honest about the choices you have made. It can be scary to admit that you have not been who were supposed to be. However, you cannot find your freedom if you do not address your past. In an interview which I did with Paul Young, author of *The Shack*, he talked about how he was caught in a lie by his wife and then chose to be honest about all of the lies he had been living. For an entire 24 hours, he bared his soul to his wife, fully believing there was no way she would love him after he was honest. What he found was that she was able to truly love him without condition once he had been fully honest.

The devil wants us to believe we cannot and will not be loved if we are truly ourselves. The part he skips over, though, is that God loves us in spite of ourselves. He loves us because He loves us. We don't have to do anything to deserve it. We don't have to earn his love. We don't have jump through hoops or dance on one foot or start with everything together in our lives. What we have to do is be honest and admit that we need Him, that we were not doing life the right way without Him. It is in our weakness and need for the remodel that His power is made manifest. So, what are you waiting for? Be honest right now and admit to God that you need Him. Confess who you have been and ask for His guidance in order to be who you can be.

HOLD NOTHING BACK

One of the stories that I have always loved was about Hernando Cortes, who was an explorer and conqueror. I do realize that conqueror in today's terminology would be more like a pirate or a thief, but back then it was simply a job that one chose. What set Cortes apart from the other conquerors was his total commitment to what he was doing. Setting sail from the shores of Cuba in the early 16th century on an expedition for which he had sold most of his possessions to help fund, he set out to take down the Aztec Empire and claim the greatest treasure that was known at the time. At the last minute, the very people who had given him the rest of the funding for the trip turned against him and told him to give up. He did not listen and he continued down the path to what he knew to be his destiny. When he and his men arrived at the Yucatan Peninsula, instead of going straight to battle, he befriended a tribe from that area, successfully gaining new support for the mission and using a local interpreter, Dona Maria. He had his men visualize the victory. They spent time day and night imagining what it would be like to take the world's greatest treasure. The practiced their fighting skills. They garnered support and learned local strategy. They did not rush blindly into the new world. Instead, they had a plan.

It was on the morning that they were to go into battle that everything changed for those men though. He gathered them in, just as he had done dozens of times before. They were likely expecting a pep talk about what an awesome victory it could be. Perhaps a few of them were even thinking that he might tell them where to meet if things got too intense. That wasn't what he said at all though. The three words that he said would change the course of history, would lay claim to much of what we now know as Mexico, and demonstrate that anything can happen when you pursue success with no other options. Those three words were: "Burn The Boats!" He burned the boats that he and his men had arrived on. Now, he and his men had only two choices. They could take the treasure or they could die trying. It is amazing how much more motivated a person becomes to attain success in any endeavor when they cut off all other options.

If you cling to things from your past, you are clinging to the boats that might take you back in the other direction. It is critical you don't save the old sheetrock to put back up, or hang on to the studs that had rotted or been damaged by termites. When you hang on to the very things that have kept you from finding your success, you can never take the treasure that was meant for you in this life and the next. Burn the boats and see what God can do next. You will be truly amazed.

Moving ourselves forward and keeping on track requires that we create a burning desire, have faith, and surround ourselves with the right people. These three things will change the course of your history into the potential of your future.

CREATE A BURNING DESIRE TO LIVE INTO YOUR NEW MODEL

Why in the world do you want to live a remodeled life? Why do you want to get rid of the old and lay claim to the new? Why do you think that the old is not good enough? Those are questions that begin to light a fire inside of you. They are questions which make you face the reality of the lack from your previous life. It isn't a lack of money I am talking about, though. It is a lack of peace. By living your old life, you are living outside of the peace of God. You are living a life rooted in illusion instead of truth. Your burning desire comes from the emotional and logical reasons that you must move forward. It comes also from the emotional and logical reasons that you will suffer or have pain if you do not move forward. What I would like for you to do is to write out three reasons for each of those, to help you create the burning desire to live the remodeled life that was designed for you.

Emotional Benefits of My New Life

Logical Benefits of My New Life

Emotional Pain That Comes From Backsliding

Logical Pain That Comes From Backsliding

HAVE FAITH

Faith is the absolute belief that there is a God and that He loves you and wants the best for you. God is the great contractor for your life. He is waiting on your permission to dive into your life and make a change. He wants to get rid of the old stuff, the old habits, the old limiting beliefs, and bring in the new. He wants to help you find the best version of yourself and use that to make a difference in this world. Just like a contractor, however, He is waiting for permission. The big difference is that your contractor, God, paid the price for the remodel with His Son, Jesus. You simply have to wake up to the truth that He wants the very best for you. I use the term "wake up," because it is as though most people are drifting through life in a dream state, in an illusion. God has always been there for you, with you, and around you. Having faith in Him means giving up the need to control the illusion and allowing Him to make His power known. It is about letting go of the control factor and simply trusting. Decide right here and now that you trust your contractor. Even when the demolition is scary or when the process looks out of whack, trust God. Trust Him because you are choosing to, and don't let go of that choice!

SURROUND YOURSELF

One of the reasons that we have stayed in the old version of ourselves for so long is that we have surrounded ourselves with people who were in that same stuck pattern. One of the more challenging things that we do is surround ourselves with people who have already remodeled their lives and are living in the wholeness of God. Joining a small group, an accountability group, or a church where you are given the things you need in order to grow and develop will set you on the path to remodel success. If you were replacing your air conditioning system, you wouldn't want to remove the old duct work and then simply put it back in. You would want, and need, all-new duct work. You would need to fill your lungs with fresh air that would keep you healthier. The same thing is true for your life. The people who kept you in the version of yourself you are trying to remodel will not bring you the new life you are seeking. Find people who are remodeled and try to add value to their lives. Spend your time helping others continue to grow and succeed and your remodel will go much faster!

5 REPAIR THE STRUCTURE

When someone desires to live a more fulfilled life, they start with a structure that can support the future that they desire. Max Lucado, in his book *On The Anvil*, teaches about the purification of our lives by the fire of trials. Repair can sometimes be a painful process. We face the challenges of our neuropathways (thought patterns) pulling us back to our previous thoughts. We struggle with building depth in our beliefs. We face the reality of our old life wanting to come back in. In Lucado's book, he discusses the impurities in our lives that are purified by the fire. We are often upset by the fact that we are facing struggles and even cry out to God asking, "Why is this happening to me?" We forget, though, that it is the struggle that builds strength. It is the fire that removes impurities. It is the new foundation God is putting together through us that provides a stronger manner of standing against temptations.

When a person is overcoming an addiction, they know that the foundation must be based on new beliefs and new thoughts that support the new way of living. We cannot live a fully charged life with faulty wiring. There are things in each of our lives that are solid and things in our lives that are in desperate need of repair. If we live under the illusion that everything is perfect, without taking a closer look, then we will often be disappointed in our outcomes. The electrical wiring in a house can either provide a lighted pathway for a person whenever they need it or it can burn the house down if it isn't good. The walls, support beams, and framework of the house can either hold up the roofline which covers your family, or it can drop on you and your family and take everything. Rebuilding the right way is critical because it either puts you back in your old life (done wrong) or puts you into a new life (done right).

As you begin to repair your life, look at everything—and I do mean everything. You cannot just look at removing one thing, although it is often best to prioritize what needs to come out. You also have to look at what to add in. Just removing things from your life doesn't create a better life. You will have to replace things in order to actually rebuild. Be relentless about inspecting the things that make up who you are. The wall structures, the support beams, the wiring, the floor joists, the rafters, and everything in-between have to go through a thorough examination when redoing a home. Your thought patterns, behavior, friends, places you hang out, things you do, movies you watch, and music you listen to are all a part of the foundation of your life. It is only in exposing these things to light that the potential pitfalls can be taken care of.

The electrical structure of your life is represented in your thoughts. After all, thoughts are simply electrical impulses that are telling the body what to do and when to do it. If you find that you are doing things that are not right, don't blame your eyes or your hands or your feet. Instead, look at what controls the eyes and the hands and the feet. When you look at your thought life, you are looking at the manner in which your neuropathways are structured. You are looking at the habits you have formed that make up your life. Charles Duhigg, in his book *The Power of Habit*, discusses how the habit loops that are created run in a separate part of the brain from conscious thought. People begin by choosing to do something as a result of a triggering event. They choose this response to the trigger over and over again until one day, they just react to the trigger without any conscious thought whatsoever.

Think about this from the perspective of being a Christian. In the beginning of building your new structure, it seems like you keep having to choose to be a good person. Something happens and you initially want to go backwards or misbehave because that is what seems natural, but you discipline yourself to do the right thing, to be nice, to hold your tongue, etc. It seems ridiculously hard at first, but it does become easier and easier, as long as you continue making the same right choices. The old neuropathways don't go away. Instead, Duhigg says that we simply create a loop around them. I think of it like many of the small towns that exist in the panhandle of Texas and West Texas. The Texas Department of Transportation keeps building loops that go around and over these small towns. They aren't getting rid of the towns or the old roads that went through the towns. They are simply bypassing the old town. What this has done, however, is make it very difficult for the old town to keep existing. It has removed the energy that goes into the town and removed the traffic as well. When you ignore something long enough, its fire goes out. We want to get away from the old thought life long enough to create a new thought life and a new belief system. We need a super-highway which bypasses the old town that doesn't offer us anything of value anymore.

As we spend time rewiring our habits, we are building up the walls of support at the same time. Our support walls are those friends who will support our desire to be better, to live a remodeled life. One of the big struggles we often have is that our old support walls were the very things that kept us in the life that we were in. It is our new support walls that allow us to give up the limiting beliefs and behavior that held us back. When a porch is sagging, my crew and I have to lift it up and then put in a brace before we remove the old support posts and replace them with new and stronger ones. Your life is no different. Think about the places where you are not leveled out. Think about where you need to be propped up and supported in order to let go of the old beliefs that were rotting away who you are. Consider the idea that these things can be eliminated, but only through the process of being lifted up first and then removing the old posts and finally putting in newer and stronger supports for your life. This process of repairing the structure of your life is where the change begins to become permanent and you begin to be truly intentional about who you will be next.

THE BIG THREE

In order to create a strong foundation, the following three things must be examined and repaired in our lives:

1. The foundation of our beliefs: You have to know and believe that God loves you and that you are blessed. His only request is that you open the door and allow Him to be in relationship with you. God isn't angry at you. He is longing for a relationship with you. The distinction between Legalism and True Freedom begins to reveal itself with this component.
2. The structure of our habits and behavior: As

amazing as it is to understand the new way of living our lives, it is ultimately the behavior that we exhibit that others will know us by. Your outward definition in your old life rested on what people witnessed through your behavior. Your new life will be known by your new behavior as well.
3. The covering of our life (the roof that protects us): When we repair our lives, we are placing a new roof of protection over ourselves. We are placing a new truth over ourselves. We are surrounding ourselves with people and inputs that build us up continuously and do not tear us down.

THE FOUNDATION OF OUR BELIEFS

There are a number of verses that are really important for you to understand in order to embrace the remodeled version of yourself. I have put together my own collection that builds the foundation of right belief in my life. It is critical to understand that God has given us a pathway toward wholeness and restoration. The challenge for most people is letting go of the self-determinism and taking hold of the truth that God has provided. It is in surrendering to God that we will finally feel in control of our lives.

> Hebrews 11:1 (NLV): Faith is the confidence that what we hope for will actually happen; it gives us assurance about things we cannot see.

Faith is difficult for anyone that does not trust in God. Faith is the willingness to simply let go of needing to control everything in your life and knowing that God is in control. To have faith, we must trust, which means that we must let go of controlling our situations and allow God to do His work through us. We have to have absolute confidence in God being in control of our lives. There is so much freedom from stress and struggle when you allow God to work, and you stop judging the things in your life as God trying to punish you or the world being out to get you. God has your back, and he is strangely accommodating to your success. He truly wants you to find success and peace and joy. God is the very fiber of your existence. He is bigger than you, bigger than your struggle, and bigger than anything that might come against you. Let go and have faith that He loves you and wants you to be successful.

> Ephesians 2:8 (NLV): For by His loving-favor you have been saved from the punishment of sin through faith. It is not by anything you have done. It is a gift of God.

Grace is not something that we can earn. You cannot feed a certain number of homeless people and then be saved. You can't say a certain number of prayers and be saved. You can't do anything to earn salvation. You are saved because you have returned to the tree of life. If you tried to earn your way into heaven, you would need limitless lifetimes to try, and would still fall short of being able to earn salvation. John Wesley (the founder of Methodism), on his trip back from America to England and after failing miserably as a minister to convert anyone in America, found himself in the midst of a horrible storm at sea. He was on a boat with a group of Moravians who were unafraid of death for they knew, through faith, that they were saved. Despite the fact that Wesley had spent 13 years in the ministry and most of his life studying the Bible, he felt unloved and unworthy because he did not understand grace. As he asked several of the Moravians how they could sing and worship and be at peace with the possibility of not surviving the journey home, they responded by explaining grace to him. Grace is the acceptance of the truth that God is always with us, always a part of us, and has always wanted the best for us. Grace is knowing that there has never been a time that God was apart from us. The fear of the afterlife comes only from the fear that God is not with us. Grace is the truth revealed to us that God has always been and will always be the very fiber of our existence. Your house is strong when you know and accept that you are loved because you are loved. There is no reason necessary. It is God's choice to love you no matter what.

> James 2:17 (NLV): A faith that does not do things is a dead faith.

The reason you need to understand faith and grace before you understand what to do is that it was never the doing that saved you. It was faith in God through Christ and the acceptance of God's love through grace that saved you. If you have ever been in a relationship where you loved another person so much that you would literally be willing to die for them, then you know that you would desire to do things to deepen and protect the relationship itself. The same thing is true with your relationship with God. When you in a relationship with God, you and God both want the very best for each other. You want to please each other. Because of that desire, you study God's word and you do things to demonstrate His love for everyone. You do things for other people because you have become an extension of God's grace into this world. You do because you want to, not because you are required to. That fundamental difference in the motive behind your action makes all the difference in the world when it comes to your authenticity.

> Hebrews 11:3 (NLV): Through faith we understand that the world was made by the Word of God. Things we see were made from what could not be seen.

I want you to think about this verse for a few minutes. The things that make up this world are made from the things that cannot be seen. The invisible makes up the visible. Bernard Haisch, in his book, *The God Theory*, demonstrates that science has proven the existence of God from the perspective of quantum physics. God is the very energy that makes up the subatomic particles that make up the atom, which is the building block of all that can be seen in the universe. This means that the very existence of reality is based solely on the very existence of God. Deepak Chopra describes this energy as the thinking non-stuff that creates quantum reality. The intelligence that is God and that makes up all that exists is what connects everyone to everyone else and to everything else. This connected intelligence is what helps us to understand the foundational truth that "God *IS!*" God is all that exists. God is everywhere, everything, everyone. God is the loving truth that makes up reality and therefore can never be separated from you, because He is the very existence of you.

> Galatians 5:22-23 (NIV): [22] But the fruit of the Spirit is love, joy, peace, forbearance, kindness, goodness, faithfulness, [23] gentleness and self-control. Against such things there is no law.

Think about the trees you have seen in your life. If you have ever had an apple tree in your yard or seen an apple tree, you would assume that it is an apple tree from the top to the bottom. You would even assume that if you removed the apples from it and stapled other fruits on it that it would still be an apple tree. However, you first recognized it by the fruits that were coming from the tree. Because you have your roots in faith in God and in the grace of your salvation, you will naturally produce fruit that is pleasing to God. If you have not produced or are not producing fruit that is pleasing to God, then you must step back and re-examine the roots of who you are. This is going back to the wiring and the foundation and the very structure that is now you. If those are right, then you will naturally exhibit love, peace, patience, kindness, gentleness, and self-control. No law has ever been created—nor will one ever be created—that could or would go against these fruits. To love is to neither fear nor judge. We are called to love. This means that we are called to create peace. This means that we are to be patient with one another in love. This means that we are to be gentle in our words and deeds towards and with others. This means that we are to patiently love one another and give others time to find their connection to God. This means that we are to control our attitude, our tongue, our actions, our complete self. The person who cannot control their actions is the person who has submitted to the ego instead of to God. Self-control is the demonstration that we can allow God to be God and we can accept our role as His hands and feet on this plane.

> Philippians 4:6-7: ...Therefore [6] Do not be anxious about anything, but in every situation, by prayer and petition, with thanksgiving, present your requests to God. [7] And the peace of God, which transcends all understanding, will guard your hearts and your minds in Christ Jesus.

There is no need for you to be worried, anxious, timid, wound up, put out, turned off, angry, or any other out-of-control emotion anymore. You are loved and cared for and a child of God. This means that your foundation is in that relationship alone. The rest of your existence is dependent upon that understanding alone. The rest of who you are is based on God's connectedness to you. What reason do you have to be anxious if you are made up of the very "thinking non-stuff" that is God? What reason could you possibly think of to worry if you know that God has your back and wants you to grow in the fullness of Christ's love? If you know that you are to face trials in order to strengthen you, then why are you worried about going to the "gym of life" in order to allow God to "Pump…You Up?" Let go of the need to control everything and trust in God and all of your anxiety disappears. I do not pretend to understand everything. The beauty of knowing that God is always with me is in knowing that I don't need to understand everything. I simply need to listen to God and immerse myself in the Word of God in order to find the path that God has laid out for me.

THE STRUCTURE OF OUR HABITS

There are some very specific habits which will help you reinforce the foundation and new wiring that is the new you. The first thing you must do is choose to be grateful. Paul, when he was in prison, talked about how he had learned to be content in any and all circumstances. He had learned to choose a faith in God and a faith in what would come next. He separated his worth from his circumstance. Every day, Paul was able to wake up and see the beauty in his situation, even when his situation was one that the world would see as dismal. It is not your circumstance that determines your happiness. It is your choice that determines your happiness. First thing every morning, write down three things that you are thankful for in a journal. Last thing every night, write down three things from your day that you were thankful for. In the morning, you are focusing on a general gratitude and at the end of the day, you are focusing on a gratitude for the day itself. If you choose to look for things to be thankful for, you will always find them. If you choose to look for things to be upset about…well, you will always find them. Choose every single day to look for the good and you will become the good.

The second habit we must have is that of demonstrating the Love of God in this world. This is what I would refer to as "random acts of kindness." We are called to be the hands and feet of Christ. This means that we are given the opportunity to be the embodiment of God's Love every day. Drew Dudley, in a TED Talk given in Toronto Canada, talked about the importance of everyday leadership. He tells a story of simply passing out candy to incoming freshmen at the university and making people smile and laugh. He did not remember the specific situation that he recounted; it was a regular act that he performed. His story relates to someone coming back to him years later and thanking him for his kindness and letting him know that he was the reason that she was going to finish her studies, as well as the reason that she had found the man that she would marry. He talks about how much he wishes he could recall the specific incident because it was such a cool story. He could only retell the story that she told him though. What we do on a daily basis does make an impact. Every encounter that we have with another person will leave them either better or worse. The interactions that you have are your choice. Who and what will you choose to demonstrate every day? Will you do good things for others or will you be self-absorbed? Random acts of kindness demonstrate God's love without expecting anything in return. That is the embodiment of God's love for us. He demonstrates His love for us and did so by sending His son to die for us while we were still sinners. He did not require us to change before He loved us! We are to do the same.

The third habit that you must be in is that of immersing yourself in God's word daily. When you put good things into your mind and your heart, then good things are reflected into the world. We are called to be a mirror for Christ's love. Christ is God's light shining in this world. He aimed Christ's love at us. If we are a mirror, then we will reflect and amplify that love. We receive the light through studying God's word. What is truly amazing is that I have read the Bible cover to cover more than once and still find things in the Bible, that I need right now, which I did not notice the last time I read it. The Bible is God's Word breathed into us. It is the mouth-to-mouth resuscitation that brings life back into us and allows us another chance to go into the world and share the good news of Christ. The Word of God gives us strength to have faith, understanding to embrace the peace of God, and fuels the continued remodelling within our lives. When you study the Word of God daily, you are partaking of the Bread of Life. Think about this for a moment: If you don't feed yourself, you can survive for a while, but eventually you will die. Your spirit is a living thing. If you do not feed it well, then it dies. Eating the wrong things makes your spirit unhealthy. Eating the right things, the Word of God, makes it healthy and strong and vibrant. What you consume is a choice that becomes a habit. Choose the Word of God daily and embrace the habit of eating from the fruit of the Tree of Life.

THE COVERING OF YOUR LIFE

Many of us…ok, the vast majority of us strive to have a roof over our heads and food in our bellies. Laying the right foundation in belief and then having the right habits to build a structure gives us the ability to keep the right roof over our heads. The roof that covers you is the accountability of the right friends and associations in your life. When you remove an ember from the fire and place it outside of the fire, it burns for a short time and then goes out. When it is placed back in the fire with other embers, it is rekindled and begins to fulfill its purpose again.

You need the fellowship of other believers. I hear

over and over again that people don't want to go to church because there are so many hypocrites there. As Zig Ziglar said, "If a hypocrite is between you and God, then the hypocrite is closer." There are hypocrites, sinners, and strugglers everywhere you will go in this life. They are seeking ways to find the truth as well. Many of them have not yet established the right foundation of understanding and are therefore trying to rely on themselves instead of God. You are not called to force all people to believe. Instead, you are called to bear witness to the Good News of Christ. This means you are called to live a connected life, connected to God. You will need other people in your life to help you, to hold you accountable when you slip up, to encourage you as you recover, and to love you when you fail. Find other Christians to connect with, who are also seeking to live into the fullness of God's Love. As Proverbs 27:17 (NIV) says: "As iron sharpens iron, so one man sharpens another."

It is not easy to submit yourself to be accountable for the fruits that you produce. It is a choice that you make, and one that cannot be made for you. Your choice to be in fellowship with other believers is one that will push you to be a continuously better version of yourself. It will push you to deepen your beliefs, change the wiring of your thoughts, and bear fruit that builds a strong house. By intentionally putting other strong Christians in your life, you are able to cover yourself and expose yourself to good thoughts, the right pathways, and great examples of how to demonstrate God's Love. You have a much easier path to living in faith and connectedness when you associate with other people who are going to the same place as you. Cover yourself with other people who build you up and do not tear you down.

6 SHEETROCK—THE CANVAS

The life that we live moving forward is a blank canvas. We have the chance to paint something beautiful. We can choose the texture of our lives, just like choosing the texture of the finish on our sheetrock. We can choose the paint color, or how we will add beauty to the world. We can choose our decorations, or how others will know us from now on. What we choose to do with our lives is completely up to us.

When I see the blank canvas of a house coming back together, I get very excited because it signals the opportunity to make something incredible which has both a strong foundation and an outward beauty. During this phase of your DIY project, you have to inspect the model you created and overlay that model on your canvas. This process helps you know if what you began with is the real desire of your heart. Even though you started with a vision, now is the time to establish the goals that you have for your life.

It can be difficult at times to know if you are on the right path when you just set a goal and start working toward it. Instead of jumping straight into the goals, you have to begin seeing the completed picture on the canvas of your life. The process of visualizing your future helps you to know for sure that it is the future you want, as well as helping you begin to embrace the future as your own. When you completely clear your mind and then slowly allow the picture of the end result to come into focus on the canvas, you begin to accept that new future instead of fighting against it.

Trust me on this one; there are things in this world that will fight against you fulfilling your destiny. That is why it is so important to be able to grasp on to the future that is in front of you and the possibilities for success that exist. Everything exists in your beliefs first. Until you believe something, it cannot come into existence. I have, at times, thought back to what it must have been like to be a great explorer, someone like Christopher Columbus. I think about how he had to keep his men focused on the future which he knew existed. I think about the beliefs that he must have held on to in order to maintain his focus and his drive. I would imagine that he did the following every day before dawn.

> *Today is the day that I find new lands. Today is the day that I prove that the world is not flat, but rather it is round. Right now, I clear my mind of all clutter, of all noise, of all distraction. I see nothing but complete white, a blank canvas on which I can paint any future that I desire. I let go of my past. I let go of mistakes. I let go of struggles. I let go of pain. I embrace that right now, this moment, the present moment, is all that matters. I am beginning the first day of the rest of my life and I am the master painter that can create any image that I desire. As I begin to fill in the canvas, the blank canvas that has endless possibilities, I see land coming into sight. I see my*

crew and me smiling and laughing as we congratulate one another on finding a new world, on proving that the world can be conquered from any direction. I feel the emotion of joy and pride and fulfilled dreams as the picture is more and more complete. The ocean becomes clear and calm. The land is made out in perfect detail. There are people in this new land that welcome us with open arms, that are glad to see us. There are new plants, new animals, new opportunities everywhere I look. As the picture fills in with clarity, I see that this was the picture of my future all along. I am filled with peace as I see the future I knew was always mine. I am filled with hope as I accept the fact that this picture is filling in more and more each and every day. I know that the picture painted on this canvas is the future intended for me and that nothing can stand in the way of me achieving that future! I am at peace with the picture of my future. I am filled with hope and joy. This is the picture of my future. This is my destiny! I know that all the world conspires for my success and I am more than willing to accept its help.

Think about what it must have been like to set sail without knowing for sure that you would succeed. After all, there was no proof that things would work out. Nobody else had ever done what he was about to do. Nobody else had demonstrated before him that this could even be done. If he had died on the journey, it is likely that nobody ever would have known what happened, or even known his name. He was different though. He was filled with a vision that was so strong that he could only succeed. He never even considered the possibility of failure. Despite the fact that his men questioned the sanity of the journey regularly, he never did. As a leader, when your vision is strong enough, it can actually carry teams of people along the path with you. The simple truth is that people are desperate for someone with a vision. They need an example of what it means to be successful. They need an example of what it is like to have no doubt you will win at something. When you see that blank canvas, then fill it in with the possibilities of the future, you are finding your path to success. You are painting a picture of what could be. You are filling in the possibilities for others to accept. The most amazing thing happens when your vision is strong…People go out of their way to help you! They want to see someone overcome the odds and succeed. They want to see someone live into their potential. They love seeing you go from blank canvas to full potential.

This means that the first step in setting and attaining your goals is to develop reverse paranoia. This is the process of believing that the world is "out to help you" instead of "out to get you." If you will wake up every morning and begin with the following mantra, the process of setting and attaining your goals will be significantly easier.

> "I know that the entire universe is on my side. God has a master plan for me to prosper, to succeed, to be happy, and to spread light wherever I go. Everywhere I go, people try to make my life better. They want me to succeed even more than I want to succeed in living a new life! I welcome their help and accept my positive and awesome future now."

The mantra is to remind you that you are not alone. You are in this with friends, family, enemies, and strangers. God can and does use anyone and everyone—yes, I said anyone—to make your life better. God will use even your enemies to arrange fantastic opportunities for you to live the life you desire and which God has planned for you. You just have to be open to those miracles.

Once you get it in your mind that the world is out to help you, you have to create a roadmap for your success.

A destination without a plan is just a hope. And hope, my friends, is not a strategy. Every goal that you set must have the following components:

- Specific
- Measurable
- Action-oriented
- Realistic
- Time-defined

The SMART goal system is not new, but it is very effective. The first component of this system is to get specific. There are variations between fuzzy goals and specific goals. For example, a fuzzy goal would be that you want your house remodeled, or that you want to use a pretty color of paint on the walls. There is no real way of knowing whether the goal was attained or missed because we don't know how to define the goal itself.

Do the following exercise: Take a piece of paper (I prefer a 4-by-6 notecard) and place it on the top of your head. Take a pen and without moving the paper, draw your dream home on the paper. Put as much detail as you can into the drawing; just draw it while the paper is still on your head. This means that you are not able to look at the picture as you draw it. After a few minutes of drawing your dream home, take the paper and have a look at your masterpiece. Is that the drawing you would take to me, your builder, and say, "Can you build this for me? It is my dream home and I want it built just like this!" If you are like most normal people, the answer to that question would be an emphatic "NO!" We don't want something different. We want the actual thing that is in our head. So, begin with some real specifics. If your objective for your life is to pay off all of your debt, then you need to say: "My goal is to pay off all of my debt and not attain any new debt." It is easy to understand what that means. If the goal is to buy a new car/truck, then your goal has to be: "My goal is to buy a brand new Chevrolet 2500, four-wheel-drive, four-door pickup, with a white exterior and a tan leather interior, with the largest engine possible, and the best stereo available in a new Chevy 2500 truck." That is much more specific than, "I want a new truck."

Once you have the specifics down, you have to ensure that it is measurable. This means that there have to markers along the way. When I remodel, I set the measurables as the sub-goals attained along the way so that we know that we are on the right track. If the objective that we are going after is to remodel your home, then we have to say that we will remodel your home by finishing the kitchen and the bathroom in 45 days, and will transform the kitchen and bath from where they are right now to look new and match the drawing that our designer put together. You have to have the map for how you will measure your success. If we are not measuring against the drawing that we worked up before we started, then what are we measuring against? If we just say that it will be different, that is easy. We could just punch some holes in the walls and call it a day. That would, after all, be different from what you have right now. It would not, however, be what you actually wanted. It would just be different.

The third component of great goal setting is to make it action-oriented. This means that everything we define has to be focused on what we will do in order to achieve our results. If you are talking about remodeling your life and your goal is to go from 198 pounds to 185 pounds in four months, then you would state it like this, with the action component included: "I am going from 198 pounds to 185 pounds in 120 days by reducing the amount of food I eat, cutting out soft drinks, energy drinks, and high-calorie coffee drinks completely, and by adding 40 minutes per day of cardio exercise, seven days per week." Your goal has to result in you doing something different from what you are doing right now. You cannot get to where you want to be by doing what has you in the spot that you want to get out of. This is true of anything that we want to change in our lives. Action is the bridge between the goal and the attainment of the goal. What will you do? That is the question.

Some people go over the top on their goals. They say things like: "I will lose 112 pounds in the next 7 days!" Or: "I will fix every aspect of my life this month." While I do like to see people accomplish incredible things, making things unrealistic simply sets you up for failure. Once you write out your goals, ask yourself if you believe that you can accomplish it. If you can't believe it, you can't achieve it. Set goals that will challenge you to be your very best, but make sure that they are actually possible as well. You need to make sure you can win at life while still growing and achieving great things. This means you have to know that you are willing to give up what is necessary to achieve what you desire. If you are not willing to put in the work, then you will not achieve your desired outcomes.

This brings us to step number five. If it is not defined by each of the steps connected to a timeframe, it will be very easy to get off track. I begin by thinking from the end back to the beginning. I look at each step in the process and I define how long it should take to complete that step. If you don't account for each of the steps and the time required for each step, then you will often get to the end of your timeframe and realize that you are only a couple of steps into a seven-step process. Your time-defined goal on a remodel should be something like this: Along the way, we will have the tear-out done in three days, will assess the framework and patch anything necessary in two days, will redo the wiring and plumbing in four days, and will begin the remodel work of putting it together immediately following that. The entire process will be completed on or before the 30th day of work. If we don't have timelines in place, then we will get off track quickly and easily.

Putting together your goals in the SMART goal model sets you up for success in remodeling your life. With each of the aspects of the vision and goals you have created throughout this process, you have to map out how you are going to get there. On the next page is a SMART goal worksheet which you can use as a model for achieving your objectives.

Goal/work priority:

Success criteria:

Link to personal plan:

Target completion date:

Quick Review:

Specific
Focus on specific results rather than on general or vague actions. Simple goals ensure clarity. Complex goals should be broken into sub-goals. Be clear about what you want to accomplish. An objective that is too general will require more action steps than are effective.

Measurable
To determine how well a goal has been achieved, the results should be quantitative (measures amount of output) and qualitative (measures how well the task was done). How will you know when you have been successful? What are the indicators of success? You should be able to monitor and gauge progress in objective terms.

Action-oriented
The best goals are challenging, realistic, and achievable. They focus on the significant contributions (actions) required to meet your goals. Be realistic about how much you can accomplish in a given time frame (year, month, or day). Too often we set ourselves and our work teams up for failure because our expectations are too high, given the amount of time, skill, or resources we have for accomplishing a goal.

Realistic
Goals must align with and support the goals of the department, the division, and the organization as a whole. Employee goals should meet or exceed the needs of all parties, including internal and/or external customers.

Choose goals that are important for you to strive for in your work and those that will have the most impact in your workplace and your life. The objective should relate directly to your personal life objectives.

Time-Defined
A specific target date for achieving each goal should be set. Time frames ensure a proactive approach toward achieving results. You should be able to track progress against specified time frames.

7 COLOR MY FUTURE

Your future has not been written yet. Your past no longer exists. The gift you have been given is your present. In this present moment, you get to choose who you will be. Your future depends upon the endless string of present moment decisions that you make. Your past will be known by each of those present moment decisions. You get to choose. You get to choose what your life will look like.

In several of the homes that I have remodeled, the home was ugly when I got started. It had giant flower wallpaper in the living room, or an orange shag carpet, or ugly cabinets, or mismatched tiles, or half-done work. Any of those things that were bad could be chosen, one at a time, to change. When my guys would chip away tile from the 50s and replace it with hardwood or more modern tile, it would change the house altogether. As you color your future, you are now laying out the things that will matter the most for you. You are creating your priorities, which are the things you will be known for.

When I first started in business as a 20-year-old, I didn't do a lot of planning. I would wake up every day and simply hope for the best. As you can imagine, I am not in that business anymore. I have changed businesses several times over the years. It was not until I got my act together and learned to create priorities for each of my days as well as for my life that I began to experience success. When I look back on the choices I made during those early businesses, I realize that it was the lack of clear priorities that lead to the off-color lack of success I experienced. When you think about the SMART goals you just set, you begin to realize that the goal is your compass, but you still have to color every moment of your day with the right priorities in order to achieve success.

In Jon Gordon, Dan Britton, and Jimmy Page's book, *The One Word That Will Change Your Life*, the authors outline the process that they went through to learn to filter their day. Each year, the authors would sit down and imagine what was most important to them in their life and what they wanted to ensure that they accomplished in the upcoming year. They started with a personal mission statement, like most people do. They then moved to a vision statement to try to become more clear. Still, it wasn't enough. It was still too difficult to know for sure if they were allowing the right things into their life and keeping the wrong things out of their life. They needed more clarity in order to filter their world for success. This pushed them to keep chipping away at the model until they finally came down to choosing a single word that they would use as their filter. For me, I have used the word "focus," and I have used the word "inspired," as well as a couple of other words, since being introduced to this concept. It has been amazing to see how the world looks different when I am filtering the world through a single word.

To me, having a single word filter that I use every day is like knowing the exact paint color with the right numbers. If a homeowner has a piece of something with paint on it and they like the color, I work with the paint company to find the closest possible match. However, if I have the label from a can of paint that has the exact paint that they are looking for, I know I am getting what I should. That is what a one-word filter is like. In every situation, you look at what you are about to do and you ask yourself, does this help me: *Insert your one word here*. I want to know that the things I choose to do every day actually move me in the right direction. I want to know that I am accomplishing the work that matters. This can only be done if I filter my activities in one way or another.

Another model that has worked for some of my coaching clients is to outline what key activities are most critical to their success on a daily basis. Once they have discovered what the five or fewer things are that matter most, they simply do the things that matter most first. If I really loved to paint, but I hated to tear out sheetrock, I still couldn't paint before tearing out the old. This isn't about what I love to do. It is about discovering what matters the most and moves me the closest to my objectives. For salespeople, they have to put on a good set of clothes and a great attitude. They have to call on potential customers, get appointments, develop and present proposals, and ask for the business. They then have to ensure that the work gets done. They know that if they skip any step, like the one where they ask for the business, they will not be successful. They have to do the things which matter the most each and every day, and so do you. What is it that matters the most in your life?

In the end, I need to be able to take the vision of the goals that I began looking at in the last chapter and turn them into reality in my mind. Our minds don't work in the future tense. They don't work in the past tense either. They only work in the present tense. That is why it is immensely important to embrace the idea that you are living in a never-ending string of present tenses as long as you are alive. This means you will need to write out the vision of your future as if it has already been attained. In order to do that, you will need to follow the process laid out next:

1. Pick a date in the future which you will use as the completion date for your remodel of your life.
2. Pull out a sheet of paper or a computer to write out your statement.
3. Begin the statement with "Today is..." and write the date you chose in step one.
4. Paint a picture with words of what your world is like having accomplished all of the goals you set for your life. Note: You may have more goals for after the date you have chosen. That is perfectly okay. Focus on the goals you have for the specified timeframe.
5. Read your present-tense vision statement to at least a dozen friends. This is not about getting their approval or even their feedback. This is about solidifying what you are accomplishing and putting it out there so that God can begin coordinating what is needed to make your remodel come to fruition.

The simple truth of where we are is this: We are exactly who we are, where we are, with what we have because we have chosen to be here. Like we discussed in Chapter 1, we must own responsibility for our place in this world. If we do not, then we will wait for the circumstance of life to control us. We will go to the paint store and say: "I will take whatever paint you give me and I will paint my house with it. It may not be at all what I want, but what say do I really have?" That is ridiculous! You would never leave the fate of your wall color to some stranger who doesn't know you, doesn't know your tastes, and doesn't have a feel for what your house is like or where you are going with it. If we wouldn't leave a simple decision like paint color to a stranger, why would we allow the circumstances of the world to dictate who we are, what we have, or what we do in this life? We definitely shouldn't!

What will you do today that will move you toward your desired future?

What will you do today that will leave a lasting impression?

What will you do every day that will make a difference in this world and leave a legacy?

What is one word you can use to filter every action that you take? How does that word represent the essence of who you are?

Answering these questions will help you to realize that you really are in control of the color of your future. That blank canvas you started with can be turned into any masterpiece you desire. You simply have to be responsible for you. You have to change your mindset to reflect an internal locus of control. You have to accept that every decision you make is a decision that you are, in fact, making. Nobody else, nothing else, and no circumstance has control of your choices. In every situation, you get to choose what your next move will be. You get to choose who you are at that exact moment.

We shy away from the future that was designed for us when we live in fear. Living in fear means caring more about the possible future than the actual present. If we are afraid of what might be, then we lose sight of who we are. Knowing that you are a child of God means that you have the power of God on your side. You have the ability to connect to all that is. God gave us the example of knowing that He is always in the present. When Moses asked whom he should say had sent him, God answered that he should tell them that "I am" had sent him. This simple statement allows us to understand that we must be in the present moment and lay claim to our personal power in order to be who we were always meant to be. It is not about who you were, who you might be, or even who others want you to be. It is always about who you choose to be right now, in this present moment. So, my question for you is: Who are you? Take a few minutes to write at least 10 "I am" statements. "I am a great father. " "I am a great contractor. " "I am a writer. " These are just a few examples. Now, write out your 10 statements that define who you are. Be positive. Claim them!

1. I am...
2. I am...
3. I am...
4. I am...
5. I am...
6. I am...
7. I am...
8. I am...
9. I am...
10. I am...

These statements will help you to keep your focus. They will remind you that you are whoever you choose to be in this present moment. You *are* because you *choose to be*. Never forget that you have a choice in every aspect of your life.

If you have followed through on the exercise, you are beginning to see a clear picture of who you will become in the future. This is not who you *could* be, it is who you *choose* to be. Claim your birthright as a child of the most high God. Claim your birthright as a co-creator with God. Then move forward and simply live into the vision you have set out before you.

8 SET THE FINAL PATH

One of the strongest lessons I learned in construction came when I was first learning to lay tile. The process of putting down tile is a meticulous one, full of artistic approach and scientific calculation. I learned that you create your plan, but then you have to be willing to adjust your cuts (your approach) as you go. Not everything fits exactly the way you imagined it in the beginning. Often times, you will have to trim a little here, shift a little there, and roll with the challenges. What is never compromised, however, is that you will complete the project. It is in making the completion of the project an absolute that we are able to set our path for the right point.

This is the part where we learn to use contingency thought along with our plan and our vision. It is also the part where we remember who gave us the vision for where we were to go in the first place. And, finally, we must be willing to remind ourselves of the importance of completing our life remodel. We have to bring the emotional and logical reasoning back to the forefront of our mind. As we go through each of the three components of setting our final path in this chapter, think back to the things you have learned in the previous chapters. We are building one new layer on top of another in order to create the new you. If you forget what you have learned, or if you choose to look away from the lessons, you slip back into the old version of yourself.

On one of the houses that I remodeled, we did a great deal of electrical work. We added outdoor lighting, added lights in a breezeway that was built, and even redid some of the wiring that was in the house already. Throughout the remodeling process, there are a number of opportunities for things to go wrong. All it takes—and all it took this time—was for one single wire to not be put into the right place for things to go wrong. Nothing burned down and no disasters happened—it is just that the light was no longer available because the wire was loose. When the homeowner called and said that all of the lights had stopped working, my electrician went to take a look. Luckily, he knew exactly where to look and had the entire thing fixed and secured within less than an hour. Our lives are the same way. If we haven't got everything in place just right, which is often the case in our lives, then we need to be aware of the potential for a faulty wire. The power was still going to the wire that was loose, but it connected to the rest of the lights and they couldn't get the power that they needed. The potential for the power stopped at that one point.

If you have a sticking point in your life, one that you keep going back to, that keeps being the emotional block for your success, then that is the point where the power stops. It is the point where the potential for God's power to do good works in you and through you is halted. Any time you find that your success is "stuck," think about the places in your life, particularly in this remodel, where there was a potential for the wiring to go back to the way that it was before. Think about the things which were holding you back before. These limiting beliefs have a habit of trying to creep back into our lives and drag us back to where we were. When you remodel your life, you are intentionally destroying those old beliefs and replacing them with new ones. From a thought standpoint, you are literally carving new neuropathways in your mind to serve as your new model of doing things. The problem is that the old neuropathways don't actually go away. They just get bypassed. They are there if you ever decide to take that detour back to a lack of success. I know what you are thinking because it was also the first thought that crossed my mind when I completed that concept. I thought about detouring back to the wrong pathway: "Why the heck would I intentionally take the wrong road?" The truth is that our subconscious mind sometimes drags us in the wrong direction until we have made the old pathway so obsolete and the new pathway so appealing that even the subconscious says, "Okay, this was a great idea after all."

LEARNING TO THINK IN CONTINGENCIES

Thinking through everything that has happened and everything that will come to be helps us to stay the course when things get tough. It helps us to accept the idea that failure is a real possibility, based on our thoughts mixed with our beliefs which result in our actions. It is actually easy to fail. The unfortunate part of failure is that often we look at it as a way to quit instead of a way to learn. There have been a number of jobs that did not go the way they were supposed to. Subs don't show up when they are supposed to show up. Workers don't take the kind of pride in their work that is necessary for me to make a profit. Homeowners get mad about things that have happened, haven't happened, or maybe was never even a part of the plan in the first place. In other words, things will go wrong on the path. If we know that things can and often do go wrong, why don't we have a plan for it? Think about this: Virtually everyone who gets married believes that they are marrying the man or woman of their dreams and they will be together forever! They don't believe that they will get divorced. However, more than half of first-time marriages end in divorce. This means that more than half of all people were wrong about their forever choice...right? Or, does it mean that more than half of the people getting married didn't think about how to handle the tough times along the way. Maybe they didn't even believe that there would be tough times along the way. That is the problem. The problem isn't the existence of problems. Rather, it is the refusal to see that there will be problems along the way and the lack of preparation of how to handle those problems.

    If you have ever played chess, you know that the key to winning isn't just making a good move right now. Instead, it is about making a good move with the understanding of all of the possible responses to that move by your opponent, then what your options are to each of those choices, then what they are likely to do, then what you are likely to do, and on and on. The person who can see all possible positions for the next five, six, seven or more moves is the player who will likely win. The key is to see into the future and know how each of the moves that are made will impact that future. For example, if you are trying to lose weight and get into shape, you will often overlook a single soft drink consumed because you cannot immediately see the impact of consuming that soft drink. With your life, most of your choices are not immediately seen or felt. They are off in the distance and will some day be felt. When things are in "some day" land, they are not on our radar. Very few contractors will outline to a homeowner the possible things that could go wrong. They might mention that things can go wrong, but they often overlook the fact that something almost always goes wrong on a job. When you are remodeling your life, this is more complex than simply remodeling a home. You have to have a contingency plan for the future, for each of the things that could possibly go wrong.

What if your family and friends don't support you or believe in your vision of the future? Are you willing to go all WOWSE on them? Will you keep moving forward With Or Without Someone Else? Have you developed the emotional energy to carry yourself forward even if they don't believe in you? In the movie *Fried Green Tomatoes*, one of the main characters adopts an alter ego named Tawanda who she calls on when she needs to learn to stand up for herself and her dreams. She begins placing speed-bump busters in her mind so that when those speed bumps do show up in life, she is able to simply roll over the top of them. When you are setting the final path for your remodel, keep in mind that the people who hung out with you when you were a turkey are not going to join you in eagle school. You have to be committed to your destination, regardless of whether or not others who were your friends before are willing to join you. When one of my friends stopped drinking completely because the drinks were owning him and his wife, he found that almost every friend who hung out with him at the bars and over beers and barbeques stopped hanging out with him. Although he was disappointed that there had not been real depth in those friendships like he once believed there was, he was completely committed to doing what was right and being who was right regardless of the decisions of others.

Write down three things that could go wrong with your remodel. Then, write out your plan to get past those things with or without the help of others.

      1. _____

2. _____

_____

_____

3. _____

_____

_____

When you think through what could go wrong and what you will do to overcome those challenges, you are ready to accomplish your final vision! Don't back down from where you know you are supposed to go. Step up and live into the new version of who you are and where you are supposed to go!

REMEMBERING WHERE THE VISION CAME FROM AND WHY WE NEEDED THE VISION IN THE FIRST PLACE

I don't know if you are like me, but you most likely have seen times in your life where you became absolutely clear about who you were supposed to be and what you were supposed to do with the rest of your life. If you are, like me, on the other side of that burning desire, there have also been times that the desire has faltered and you have lost track to the truth behind the vision. Your vision was put inside you when you came into existence. The challenges you have faced, the circumstances you have overcome, the lessons you have learned, and the people in your life, both good and bad, have helped to bring you the the doorstep of the vision that was meant for you. You were given a vision for where you were to go in life because our joy comes from purpose. God wants you to find your path. He wants you to find the thing that gets you fired up every day. He loves to see His children excited. Your vision is uniquely yours, but it was also divinely inspired. Taking hold of your vision and keeping it in front of you will help to keep you on track. Just like Peter, when he took his eyes off of Jesus as he was walking on water, he immediately began to sink. You too, sink when you take your eyes off of the vision that God put inside of you. You need this vision because it is the fuel for bringing your journey into purpose. You need this vision because it inspires you to live fully every day. You need this vision because it unlocks the vault to the real you, the authentic you.

REMEMBERING THE IMPORTANCE OF THE VISION AND COMPLETING OUR REMODEL

The value of the vision inside you is that it helps you remember what matters most in life. It helps you overlay the picture of what can be on top of the picture of what is. I recently met a young man who has started a company called Allergic to Average. I love the concept of the company. It is based on the idea that there are too many people out there striving to be okay instead of striving to be incredible. I have never had a family come to me and ask for their home to be remodeled into something that is acceptable. They don't want average. They want incredible. This is what they want even just for their home. How much more should we desire for our own lives? How much more should we strive to create an incredible vision of what can be and live every day into that vision?

As a reminder of how critical this vision is to you, I want you to write down what it will cost you if you don't live into the vision. If you stay right where you are and choose not to remodel your life, what is the potential that you are giving up? I want you to write for the next couple of minutes. Think of this as writing a letter chastising yourself for even considering not fulfilling all you are capable of!

_____

_____

_____

_____

_____

_____

_____

_____

_____

_____

_____

_____

Now that you have that pain you want to avoid, I want you to take a few minutes and write out all of the benefits for your life of achieving this vision. Think about everything you could gain if you fulfill your purpose. How much better will your life be? How much better will the lives of your family and friends be?

_____

_____

_____

_____

_____

_____

_____

_____

_____

_____

_____

_____

Ultimately, we go out of our way to avoid pain and to pursue pleasure. This means that in order to keep ourselves going in the right direction, we may very well have to be willing to kick our own butts, to inspire our own greatness, and to do it every day if necessary. Just always keep in front of you the potential loss of not pursuing your dreams and the potential gain of going after them!

You were given this vision on purpose! Go make it happen!

9 CLEANUP

I remember intensely disliking the cleanup process when I was young and working for my dad. I thought the process was tedious and it didn't really feel like the glorious act of creating. In fact, it felt like work. My dad and I might have just finished an incredible project that transformed the dull and outdated kitchen of a home into something that was modern and awesome. In my 14-year-old mind, it seemed like somebody else should be there doing that cleanup. It seemed like we should be above that. The lessons that I learned on the job, however, related to what it means to finalize a job were invaluable and have shaped the way I take care of my employees, the way I complete work for a customer, and the way I coach people for success. I learned five really important lessons related to the cleanup:

1. A job is not done until everything is cleaned up.
2. The final flaws and fixes are only revealed when the settled dust is removed.
3. Nothing that you do on a job will be remembered if you don't make things

presentable.
4. What you just did matters as much or more than what you did last week.
5. To finish with perfection is to be proud of yourself and the masterpiece you have created.

A JOB IS NOT DONE UNTIL EVERYTHING IS CLEANED UP

2 Kings 5:9-14 says:

> [9] So Naaman came with his horses and his chariots and stood at the doorway of the house of Elisha. [10] Elisha sent a messenger to him, saying, "Go and wash in the Jordan seven times, and your flesh will be restored to you and *you will* be clean." [11] But Naaman was furious and went away and said, "Behold, I thought, 'He will surely come out to me and stand and call on the name of the LORD his God, and wave his hand over the place and cure the leper.' [12] "Are not Abanah and Pharpar, the rivers of Damascus, better than all the waters of Israel? Could I not wash in them and be clean?" So he turned and went away in a rage. [13] Then his servants came near and spoke to him and said, "My father, had the prophet told you *to do some* great thing, would you not have done *it?* How much more *then,* when he says to you, 'Wash, and be clean'?" [14] So he went down and dipped *himself* seven times in the Jordan, according to the word of the man of God; and his flesh was restored like the flesh of a little child and he was clean.

This is just like us most of the time. We look at

what we must do in order to live the life that was intended for us, and we think, "I want to do something incredible for the Lord and not something mundane." We often want to do the glorious things but not the commonplace things. In my podcast interview with Shawn Bolz (http://rureal.org/27-hearing-gods-voice-in-life-and-business-with-shawn-bolz/), one of the things that Shawn shares is that when he first felt called to be in prophetic ministry, he mostly just told people that God loves them. He didn't have any incredible insights as he got started. Instead, he was called to remind people that they were loved and cared for. Had Shawn not been faithful in this, he would never have been given the chance to be such an incredible leader and an incredible man of God. I would encourage you to check out some of the resources that Shawn offers at: https://bolzministries.com/

We work on the jobs in front of us and when we are faithful in the little things, God can be faithful in the great things. Within our own lives, in order to be saved, we are not called to change and then be saved. Instead, we are called to claim a relationship with the Most High and then we will have the desire to clean up the rest of our life. Think about that. It is the same thing with a remodel. We don't paint, sweep, and scrub and then tear things out and build the new. We create the new first and then we clean it all up. Our job of cleaning up our lives requires us to walk in humility and learn to be faithful in the little things, like cleaning up and putting it all together. The big leap in our journey of getting our lives right is to become transformed. You cannot stay the new creation if you don't clean up the old habits though. This means that the job of transforming yourself really is not complete until the cleanup is done!

THE FINAL FLAWS AND FIXES ARE REVEALED ONLY WHEN THE DUST IS REMOVED

Matthew 7:1-6 says:

> [1] Do not judge, or you will be judged. [2] For with the same judgment you pronounce, you will be judged; and with the measure you use, it will be measured to you. [3] Why do you look at the speck in your brother's eye, but fail to notice the beam in your own eye? [4] How can you say to your brother, 'Let me take the speck out of your eye,' while there is still a beam in your own eye? [5] You hypocrite! First take the beam out of your own eye, and then you will see clearly to remove the speck from your brother's eye. [6] Do not give dogs what is holy; do not throw your pearls before swine. If you do, they may trample them under their feet, and then turn and tear you to pieces.

It is very tempting to begin looking at others when we have changed our own life and start to see all of their flaws. Often, smokers who quit are the most harsh and most angry when others smoke in their presence. By the same measure, those who have given their lives to God can often see all of the flaws in others without remembering to stay focused on themselves and not on judgment. We were not called to judge others. We were called to love others. There will still be things in our own lives that need to change. We won't really know what those are after a life remodel until the dust settles.

There is a "honeymoon period" that happens from the emotional high a person gets from letting go of their past life and embracing the fullness of the Love of God. The challenge with this is that it can still be very tough when we go back into the world. When we are back in the situations where we used to react harshly, we can be tempted to fall back into our old habits. Our calling is to focus on being who we are supposed to be, not on fixing everyone around us. When we focus on being a reflection of the Love of God, then others will be drawn to us. It cannot be our mission to make others change. Instead, our mission is serve as an example of what it means to live a life transformed. When you change your heart and your life, you have to keep cleaning things up and focusing on loving and forgiving yourself as well as others. When you live your life without judging others, you are allowing the dust to settle for yourself. By the same measure that you judge others, you will be judged. By the same measure that you simply love others, you will be loved. My encouragement to you is to love others without condition, the same way that Christ loved you without condition.

NOTHING THAT YOU DO ON A JOB WILL BE REMEMBERED IF YOU DON'T MAKE THINGS PRESENTABLE

James 3:1 says:

> [1] Not many of you should become teachers, my fellow believers, because you know that we who teach will be judged more strictly.

The world is full of examples of leaders, preachers, prophets, and evangelists who have fallen from grace. These men and women who began their good work and did amazing things to help people follow the heart of God ended up being remembered for their indiscretions instead of their accomplishments. When we live our lives in front of others, rest assured that people will be watching. There will always be people who want to know if we are authentic. They want to look at us as we transform from who we were to who we were meant to be. If they have not transformed their own life but feel that they were supposed to, they may be looking out for our faults. They may be watching for us to falter in our faith in order to justify why they have not moved in that direction themselves. As you remodel your life, what you present on the outside becomes just as critical as what is on the inside. With your new life, you are now being looked at as an example. Others will want to know if it makes sense for them to clean up their lives as well.

Imagine that you have not been a Christian in the past, but you become one. You begin to clean up your behavior and habits. You change the way you speak to your family, your employees, your coworkers, and everyone else around you. Then, one day you meet a preacher who drops the "F-bomb" on a regular basis, who smokes, and who says that you can do whatever you want as a Christian as long as you go to church and tithe. For young Christians, in particular, this can be a very confusing scenario. They are looking to this leader as a model of what they should be like and how they should live. If you have worked diligently to clean up your life, you have given up most of your habits, but you are mean to others, it is your meanness that will be remembered. That is what was meant in James 3:1. We will be judged more harshly because we are not seen as a leader or a role model. Take care to clean up all aspects of your life so that you can and will be remembered by all you encounter as an example of the Most High God!

WHAT YOU JUST DID MATTERS AS MUCH OR MORE THAN WHAT YOU DID LAST WEEK

James 2:14-19 says:

> [14] What good is it, my brothers and sisters, if someone claims to have faith but has no deeds? Can such faith save them? [15] Suppose a brother or a sister is without clothes and daily food. [16] If one of you says to them, "Go in peace; keep warm and well fed," but does nothing about their physical needs, what good is it? [17] In the same way, faith by itself, if it is not accompanied by action, is dead.
> [18] But someone will say, "You have faith; I have deeds."
> Show me your faith without deeds, and I will show you my faith by my deeds. [19] You believe that there is one God. Good! Even the demons believe that—and shudder.

We are not saved by our works or deeds. We are saved by the Grace that was given to us through the sacrifice that Christ made on the Cross. However, if someone tells you that they are the greatest contractor on earth and has no way of demonstrating you that they are, do you believe them? No, you don't. You, like almost everyone else on this earth, knows who a person is by what they do, not what they say. They know you by the actions you take every single day. They know you by the love you show to others. They don't know you simply by the thoughts you think or the beliefs you hold inside of you.

When you are choosing a contractor, you want to see the things that they have done, particularly the recent jobs that they have completed. You want to know what others have said about their work. The same is true of your life. Your friends want to know if you are going to behave differently as a result of your life remodeled. If the answer is no, then you were not truly transformed. The change in behavior, however, doesn't come from the requirement to change. It comes from the desire to be a new creation. When you change your beliefs, you are changing the things that you think. Speak life into yourself. Speak of loving God, of being forgiven, of claiming the promise of God in your life. Speak words of encouragement to others. Speak grace over judgment and others will see the good works that you do. If you wake up every single day with the intent to spread love and to do something good for others, then you will be known for your good works. Make doing good for others a part of who you are every day. Blessings will be on their way to you if you believe and act on the truth that you are to be a blessing to others. Go out today and do something that demonstrates the love and the grace of God!

TO FINISH WITH PERFECTION IS TO BE PROUD OF YOURSELF AND THE MASTERPIECE YOU HAVE CREATED

2 Timothy 4:6-8 says:

> 6 For I am already being poured out like a drink offering, and the time of my departure is at hand. 7 I have fought the good fight, I have

finished the race, I have kept the faith. [8] From now on the crown of righteousness is laid up for me, which the Lord, the righteous judge, will award to me on that day—and not only to me, but to all who crave His appearing.

There will always be times that living this new life is tough. There will be times when you think it would be easier, or even more enjoyable to revert back to the person you used to be. The one common thread of all great leaders, of all people who have made a positive impact in this world is this: They have faced struggles and kept the faith. Think back to math class in high school. If you had a problem to solve, and you showed all of your work, and you got the answer right, but you did not put the answer in the answer box, it would be counted off. However, if you finished the problem and put the answer in the right place, it would be counted as correct. This one simple thing mattered greatly. It was a detail of the job and it was your responsibility to take enough pride in your work that you could complete the entire task, not just part of it.

Imagine the thought that everything you do is an example. Every interaction you have with others will leave them either better or it will leave them worse, but it will never leave them the same. Everything you do is an example for someone to follow. It may be your children, your spouse, your friends, your coworkers, or even a total stranger that is paying attention to your example. It will be an witness, though! When you take pride in living a life that is truly remodeled, you are claiming your new destiny. You are demonstrating that you know that your life, your choices, your every day matters. Every single day is a chance to live the life you have chosen.

Every single day is one day closer to your last chance to live as a shining example to others. Not to be morbid, but I think about the time that I have left on this earth. As of today, the average person lives to 78.4 years old. This means that I have halfway done with my race, if I am an average person. I have only half of my life left to make a difference, to make a splash, and to live the life that I was called to live. What will you do with the life you have before you? The life that is behind you is done. The choices you made in the past were made and they cannot be undone, but you can take control of what you do next. You will be remembered for what you do from this point forward. Make it incredible! Make a splash! Let others know what it is like to live a life remodeled. Let others know what a difference it makes in your soul to be the man or the woman that you could be when you live into the fullness of the love of Christ!

FINISH THE RACE STRONG!
LIVE YOUR LIFE REMODELED!

10 WARRANTY WORK

As my friend Jody Holland teaches in his customer service program: "The measure of person is not in whether they make mistakes. We all make mistakes. The measure of a person is in how they handle mistakes and with what attitude." When we are seeking to remodel our lives, there will be things that break along the way. We will have broken beliefs. We will have mis-wired thoughts. We will discover that there is a flaw in the walls we have put up. We will even find circumstances happen which require us to fix something we really did not break on our own. The mistake that we should not make, though, is to think that we could simply work harder in order to fix things, in order to deserve God's love.

Tom Fuller, in *The John Wesley Adventure*, tells the story of how John had left England and traveled to America. He had been in ministry for 12 years when he arrived in America to "save souls and convert savages." After he arrived in America as a single man, he began preaching and teaching wherever he could. During that time, a 15-year old young lady had fallen in love with him and theoretically he had fallen in love with her as well. John second-guessed himself all the time though. He wasn't sure about whether he was ready for marriage. The girl's parents were ready to bless their life together but John kept asking around for advice. He wasn't confident in this aspect of his life and needed reassurance from person after person. This went on for months until the young lady finally lost interest in him and moved on to a more serious suitor. Without telling John, she was married to another man. When they came to church after being married, John refused to serve them communion. He was mad. This made the folks in that area mad at John. That night, he was warned that a group of men aimed to string him up the next morning. Now he was scared. He fled America and headed back to England.

On the journey back to England, he described his failure as a minister in America and his brokenness from the experience. His journal told of how he worked so hard to make people believe but it simply did not work. He was feeling sorry for himself and was wallowing in the sorrow of his failure when a great storm came upon them. Now the very boat that John had climbed on with a group known as the Moravians, was likely going to sink. In his mind, he knew that he had been a failure and that he was not worthy of God's love. He feared that if he died right then, he would go to hell for all of eternity. At the high point of his self-pity, he began to hear singing. The Moravians were singing praises to God. They were not afraid. They were not worried that things were not going to work out. They were simply not scared. John was so confused by what was happening that he wobbled his way through the boat on the rough sea in order to find out what these people knew that he didn't know.

Think about this for a moment. This group of people had already remodeled their lives. They had stripped out the old wiring, the old foundation, the old everything, and built it all new. John, though, had tried to use the old wiring in the new house. He asked several of them what they knew about God. He asked them why they were so calm and could sing praises in the midst of impending doom. They shared their insights on the grace of God with him. They taught him, in the midst of the storm, that God's grace is sufficient. They taught him that one should good works precisely because they are filled with grace. People are not filled with grace because they do good works, though. As he learned from them and sang with them, he began to understand that he didn't need to "do" in order to be saved. He needed to "accept" instead. He needed to accept God's grace and love and mercy. He asked the leader of the group to pray with him and help him to have Christ in his life the way that they did. In John's journal, he describes a "strange warming of his heart" that he had never experienced before.

This was 13 years into John Wesley's full-time ministry. In the first 13 years, he had converted four people. He had taught them that they had to work their way into heaven. One had worked himself to death during that time. John had changed everything in his life except for his most important belief. He had not accepted that he was a child of the Most High God. He had not accepted that he was loved without condition. Once he got the wiring right, John Wesley went on to personally convert and save the souls of more people than any other man in ministry. The Methodist Movement grew faster than America grew during that time. It was incredible what was able to transpire once the wiring was fixed. The warranty work that God does on our lives is done out of love, not out of obligation.

When you look at your life moving forward, you have to be willing to address the following three things:

1. Faulty wiring / bad beliefs
2. Flaws in the walls—the image that others see
3. Bad hardware—things that simply go wrong

FAULTY WIRING

At the beginning of this book, you learned about the belief loop. You learned that your beliefs create your thoughts. Your thoughts create your actions. Your actions create your results. This loop has the potential for the wiring to be bad. When I first became a Christian, I knew that everyone needed to be saved. I couldn't understand why anyone would not believe the way I now believed. The funny thing is that I had not believed the right things until I was ready to accept grace for my life. When you become a Christian, when you remodel your life, you are not commissioned to annoy everyone you know who isn't living like you. Instead, you are to live as a model for what love is really like. When you go into a house that has been remodeled and looks incredible, the contractor doesn't look at you and start telling you how bad your house is. No, the house speaks for itself. It presents itself majestically before you with a living example of what it means to be all you are capable of being.

We are the same way. We are called to live as an example. We are not called to put others down or even to force them into our belief patterns. If you go into another person's house and begin trying to rip out their wires, they will remove you from the house. However, if you show them the light through your new kitchen window, demonstrate the beauty of your remodeled life and simply exist as you were meant to be, they will begin to ask you questions about how you got to the place you are in now. You don't have to make others do anything. You simply have to be the very best version of yourself, respect others for who they are, and serve as a living example of what could be. When Christ approached the woman at the well, He knew that her life wasn't right. He knew that she was living a life of sin. He didn't tell her to get things right before he was willing to accept her. He accepted her and then offered her water that would quench the thirst inside of her, thirst she could not quench with water from the well. She wanted to change because she did not have to change. She wanted to change because she knew what she was doing was not working.

People know when their wiring is off. They know when their beliefs are not bringing them fulfillment. They know when there is a hole in their hearts that can only be filled with grace from God. Had Jesus, in John 4, said, "Woman, you are a harlot and a Samaritan and I am a Jew, be gone from my sight," the woman would never have sought out the truth. Jesus was wired for love and grace and forgiveness. What are you wired for? Are you wired to be connected with God as someone whose house serves as an example of grace and love and forgiveness? My desire for you is that you will continue to upgrade your beliefs. My desire is that you will be a reflection of Christ's love for others to see. If you are remodeled into that sort of a mansion, then you will have the peace you seek.

FLAWS IN THE WALLS

Too many people put up the image that nothing is ever wrong. They pretend the world is perfect, their families are perfect, and that they never have to struggle. The truth is that the world needs authenticity more now than it ever has in the past. The world needs to see that it can live in victory by being willing to bring in help to patch the walls that are flawed. The world needs people to be authentic about who they actually are and what is actually happening to them.

Think about some of the mistakes you have made or even continue to make. Often times, people go after a leader who pretends nothing is ever wrong. Those who go around pointing fingers at others without addressing the issues that exist in their own lives are the ones the world targets first. Matthew 7: 1-3 says:

> **7** Do not judge, or you too will be judged. ² For in the same way as you judge others, you will be judged, and with the measure you use, it will be measured to you. ³ Why do you look at the speck of sawdust in your brother's eye and pay no attention to the plank in your own eye?

There is a statement I use to address my mistakes and to allow the warranty work of God to take hold. Try filling out the statement below three times (three different mistakes that you have made). Complete the following:

When I (list sin or mistake) _____,
I am loved and I am forgiven because of God's Grace and because I desire to live my life right. I am addressing this and changing the wiring so that it will not happen again.

When I (list sin or mistake) _____,
I am loved and I am forgiven because of God's Grace and because I desire to live my life right. I am addressing this and changing the wiring so that it will not happen again.

When I (list sin or mistake) _____,
I am loved and I am forgiven because of God's Grace and because I desire to live my life right. I am addressing this and changing the wiring so that it will not happen again.

We all have flaws in our walls. We have wrong outlooks towards others, wrong thoughts about ourselves, or wrong images of what it means to be a remodeled

Christian. Our goals should be to address those flaws and allow God to do His warranty work. Accept God's grace and forgiveness and change your thoughts, change your outlook, change your perspective. This will propel you in the right direction and give you the peace you desire for your present and your future.

BAD HARDWARE

We can have the best of intentions, the best of plans, and even what we believed to be the right actions, and things can still go wrong. Your hardware, or your actions in life, sometimes just don't get you the results you are seeking. I know I have put in doors that swelled and caused problems when they were not supposed to. I have installed a hot water heater that didn't heat properly. I have changed out thermostats that messed up the temperature instead of properly regulating it in a home. I took what I believed to be the right action but I did not get the right results. It can be a very frustrating experience when I did what I was supposed to do and did not get the positive results I expected. I can become angry and think that life isn't fair or I can simply take action and deal with the situation. Either way, I have work to do. I have found it to be much easier to deal with when I accept that sometimes things simply do not go according to plan. The key is to keep my focus on the end result that I am seeking and not the obstacle.

We cannot seek both the life God intends for us and the life the world would have for us. Either we serve one master or we serve the other. God's plan is for us to prosper, to be leaders, to live as a child of the Most High God. Bad hardware is to see ourselves as anything less than that, to judge ourselves by the world's standards. It is to see ourselves for anything less than the potential God has placed within us. The life we seek is a life of peace and of oneness with God. The life that the world has for us is one of comparison, one of worry, one of wondering whether or not we are good enough. This is not the life we desire. This is not what was intended.

My challenge to you, as you take the next step on this journey, is to remember that you were made from the very breath of God. You, my friend, are a child of God. As such, your birthright is to live with the peace that only being one with God can provide. Will you walk in the knowledge that God created you for a purpose? Will you walk in the confidence that you were given everything that you needed to fulfill that purpose? Will you live as the victor that God created you as? I challenge you to do just that. Live! Love! Be at peace! Fulfill your purpose!

May you be blessed in all you do! May you live in the victory of God's love! Until the next time, I am Jon Fuller, the Voice of Manifestation, a Child of God, and a remodel in progress, wishing you all the best!

Jon Fuller

ABOUT THE AUTHOR

Jon Fuller has been remodeling homes as an assistant or as the general contractor for more than two decades. He has been continuously remodeling his own life to serve God at greater levels for just as long. Jon is the host of the R U Real Podcast where he interviews guests about life, authenticity, and their journey through both gifts and setbacks. Jon actively seeks to share the gospel with those that are seeking, serves as a leader in his church, invests time in people's potential, and strives to live an authentic life. You can learn more about Jon on his website at: www.rureal.org.
You can check out episodes of his podcast at: http://rureal.org/podcast-episodes/

Made in the USA
San Bernardino, CA
06 March 2018